D1744710

Toys without Gussets

by the same author

NEEDLEWORK PUPPETS
MAKE YOUR OWN SOFT TOYS
MASCOT TOYS
FLOPPY TOYS

TOYS WITHOUT GUSSETS

Easy toymaking for everyone

by BRENDA MORTON

*with drawings by Juliet Renny
and photographs by Stephen Moreton-Prichard*

FABER AND FABER LIMITED
3 Queen Square London

First published in 1972
by Faber and Faber Limited
3 Queen Square London WC1
Printed in Great Britain by
Latimer Trend & Co Ltd Whitstable

ISBN 0 571 09948 3
(Paper covered edition)

ISBN 0 571 09861 4
(Hard bound edition)

Contents

INTRODUCTION   *page* 13

GENERAL INSTRUCTIONS

    Fabrics   14
    Stitches   14
    Stuffing   17
    Patterns   18

TOYS

Felt
    Pinky the Elephant   19
    Freddy Fir and Sally Spruce   22
    Lindy the Ladybird   27
    Leapy Frog   31
    Flutter-by the Butterfly   35
    Sea Horse   40
    Dippy Dolphin and Dilly Dolphin   43
    Polly Parrot   47

Fabric
    Chicky Chick   53
    Billy Bunny   56
    Oliver Owl   60
    Sandy Carrot   64
    Wobbly Woo and Wobbly Winnie   67

Four-legged Animals
    Timmy Tortoise   71
    Piggy Porker   75
    Rory Lion   80

Rattles
    Basic Instructions   87

1. Circular Rattle. Patterned Cotton   89
2. Circular Rattle. Embroidery   89
3. Circular Rattle. Felt Animal   89
4. Circular Rattle. Funny Face   90
5. Do-It-Yourself Shape   91
6. Bell Rattle. Felt Strips   92
7. Bell Rattle. Ric-rac   93
8. Bell Rattle. Embroidery   94
9. Bluebell Rattle   95
10. Harlequin Rattle   98

The Rupert Toys
Rupert. Basic Instructions   102
Rupert Duck   103
Rupert Cat   105
Rupert Rabbit   107
Rupert Funniman   110
Rupert Monkey   112

Glove Puppet
Jock McThistle   116

PINKY THE ELEPHANT
page 19

FREDDY FIR AND SALLY SPRUCE
page 22

LINDY THE LADYBIRD
page 27

LEAPY FROG
page 31

FLUTTER-BY THE BUTTERFLY
page 35

SEAHORSE
page 40

DIPPY DOLPHIN AND DILLY DOLPHIN
page 43

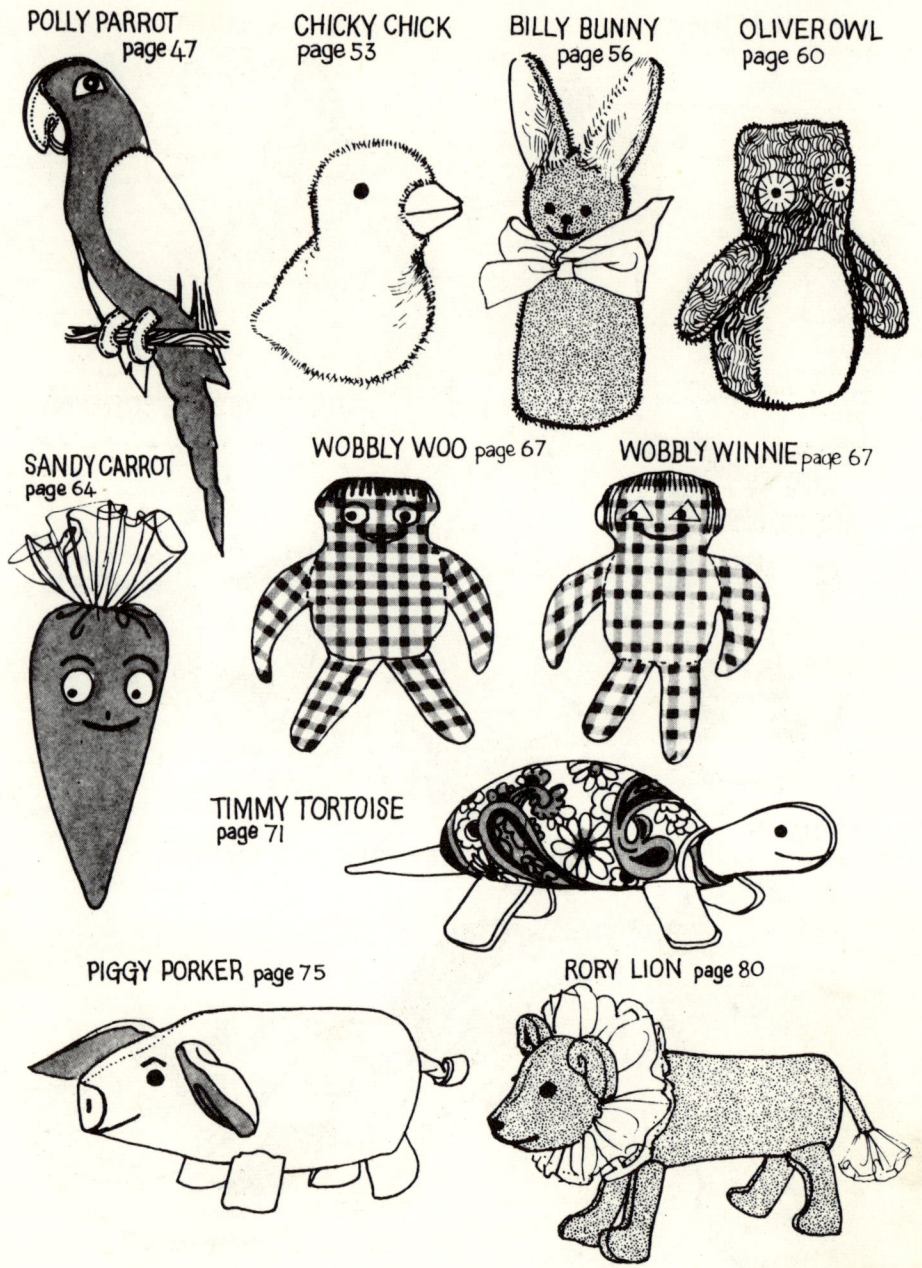

POLLY PARROT page 47

CHICKY CHICK page 53

BILLY BUNNY page 56

OLIVER OWL page 60

SANDY CARROT page 64

WOBBLY WOO page 67

WOBBLY WINNIE page 67

TIMMY TORTOISE page 71

PIGGY PORKER page 75

RORY LION page 80

RATTLES page 86

JOCK McTHISTLE
page 116

RUPERT TOYS
page 100

Rupert Rabbit   Rupert Funniman   Rupert Monkey   Rupert Duck   Rupert Cat

Introduction

These toys are very simple to make. Each toy has just two sides which are sewn together and stuffed. There are no gussets, no tucks and no complicated parts to cause difficulty.

Hesitant beginners and children will enjoy the simplicity that gives results without worry. Slow workers, or school children who only have a limited amount of time in handiwork classes, can complete them before losing interest.

Skilled workers will find that these toys make excellent contributions to a bazaar as they can be made so quickly and so economically.

General Instructions

FABRICS

There are so many types of man-made materials on sale nowadays and under so many different names that two main descriptions are used in this book. *Cotton* and *woollen cloth*. *Cotton* means any thin smooth material, whether natural or man-made. *Woollen cloth* means thicker material with a woolly, brushed or pile surface, whether natural or man-made.

Practically any type of material can be used in toymaking. So the *cotton* or *woollen cloth* terms will allow you to fit any pieces you have to the most suitable toys. Fabrics to avoid are those that fray easily, very fine ones that will show the stuffing through them, loosely woven fabrics which will bulge awkwardly when being stuffed, and thick tweeds which will not turn out easily.

Felt is used for many of the toys. It is excellent for beginners as it does not fray and is sewn on the outside.

Fur Fabric. Always lay patterns on wrong side of fabric. Cut with short snips of the scissors through the backing. When the toy is finished run a pin along the seams pulling out any pile that has been caught down.

STITCHES

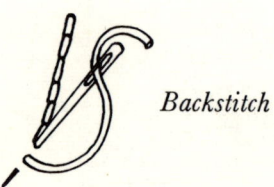 *Backstitch*

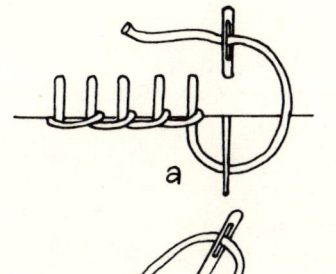

Blanket Stitch
(a) Orthodox method.

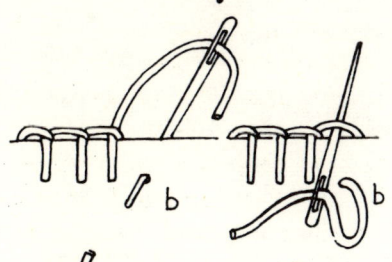

(b) Sometimes easier for small toys as left hand grips toy firmly.

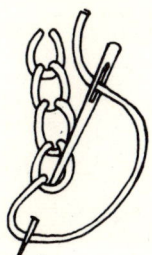

Chain Stitch
Hold thread down with left thumb. Take straight stitch from inside previous link of chain, with new thread under point of needle.

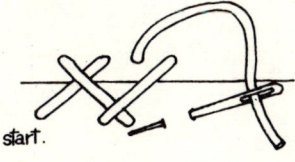

Herringbone Stitch
Small straight stitch above join, then small straight stitch below join. Needle always pointing back towards starting point.

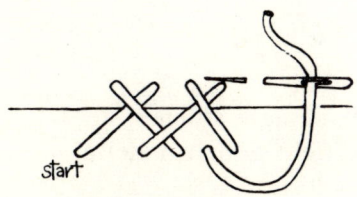

Oversewing

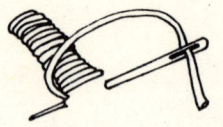

Satin Stitch
Straight stitches worked closely together.

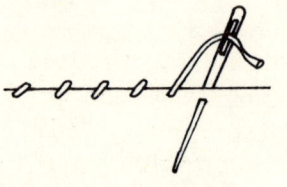

Slipstitch
Small inconspicuous stitches.

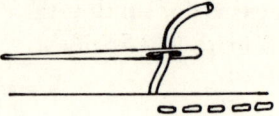

Stab-stitch
Pull the thread taut at each stage, to give smaller stronger stitches than running stitch.

Stem Stitch
As in crewel embroidery.

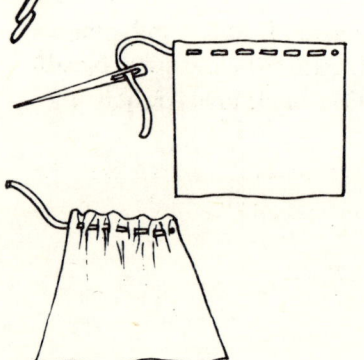

Gathering
1. Take small, straight stitches.
2. Pull thread tight so that material gathers up in folds.

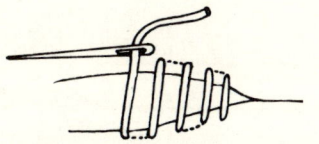

Ladder Stitch
Makes it easy to join awkward parts.

Take one small straight stitch on one part, then a small straight stitch on the other part. Keep the stitching moving in the same direction. Pull the thread tight every three or four stitches and the stitches will lace up and disappear, leaving a neat join that is very strong because there is no thread on the surface to be worn away. The diagram shows the stitches before the thread which laces it together is pulled tight.

STUFFING

Kapok and soft cotton flock are both suitable. Foam filling can be used but is more difficult to pack neatly to get a good shape and does fly around when being used.

Home-made stuffing can be made by cutting up old nylons, woollens and odd scraps of material. Cut them into very small pieces. This is usually too laborious when a quantity is needed, but if only one or two small toys are being made it provides cost-free stuffing. It can also be of value if the stuffing supply runs out in the middle of a toy.

When stuffing the toys sit at a table with polythene sheeting or a clean cloth spread on it.

1. Stuff the most difficult corners of the toy first. Then fill the corners farthest from the stuffing hole. Work gradually back to the hole itself.
2. Put only a small amount of stuffing in at a time. Press it firmly into position before adding more.
3. Keep the toy firm. But remember it is a soft toy and do not press the stuffing so hard that the toy feels as though it had been made of iron! It may split if you do.

Diameter
1 cm (½ in) 25 cm (10 inches)

Not essential, but a great help. Make one from a piece of dowel rod, rounded at one end and sharpened to a blunt point at the other. Or use a thick knitting needle. Use it to guide stuffing into narrow parts and far corners.

PATTERNS

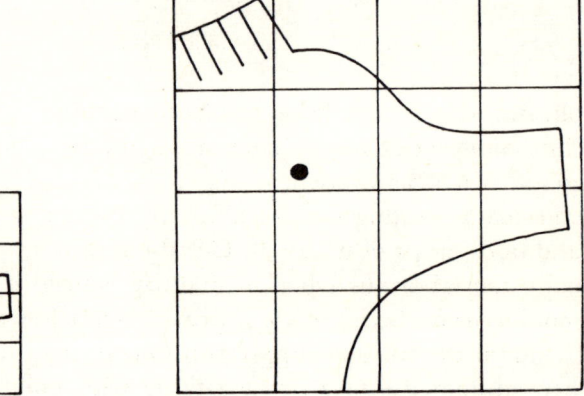

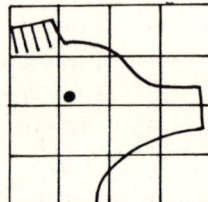

All patterns shown on lined squares must be increased by this method.

Take a sheet of paper. Rule lines across it, 2 cm apart. Then rule lines down it, 2 cm apart. This covers the sheet with 2 cm squares.

The printed diagram is covered with tiny squares. Copy the pattern shapes carefully on to the same number of squares on your ruled paper. Cross the lines at exactly the same places. In this way you finish with an identical shape and one that is the correct size for the toy.

You do not need to be an artist. Just follow the line carefully from square to square.

To get accurate patterns, squares must measure 2 cm. This is one occasion where a conversion to inches will not work properly!

Pinky the Elephant

This elephant does not stand. It is a small toy for a young baby to hold. For a baby boy make BLUEY THE ELEPHANT using pale blue felt with royal blue ears.

MATERIALS

Pink felt, two pieces each 17 cm × 12 cm (6¾ in × 4¾ in); red felt, two pieces each 7 cm × 4 cm (2¾ in × 1½ in); *thread*, machine twist, pink and black; kapok or soft cotton flock.

PATTERN

Body. Trace pattern. Cut two pieces in pink felt.
Tail. Cut one piece, 4·5 cm × 3·5 cm (1¾ in × 1¼ in) in pink felt.
Ears. Trace pattern. Cut two pieces in red felt.

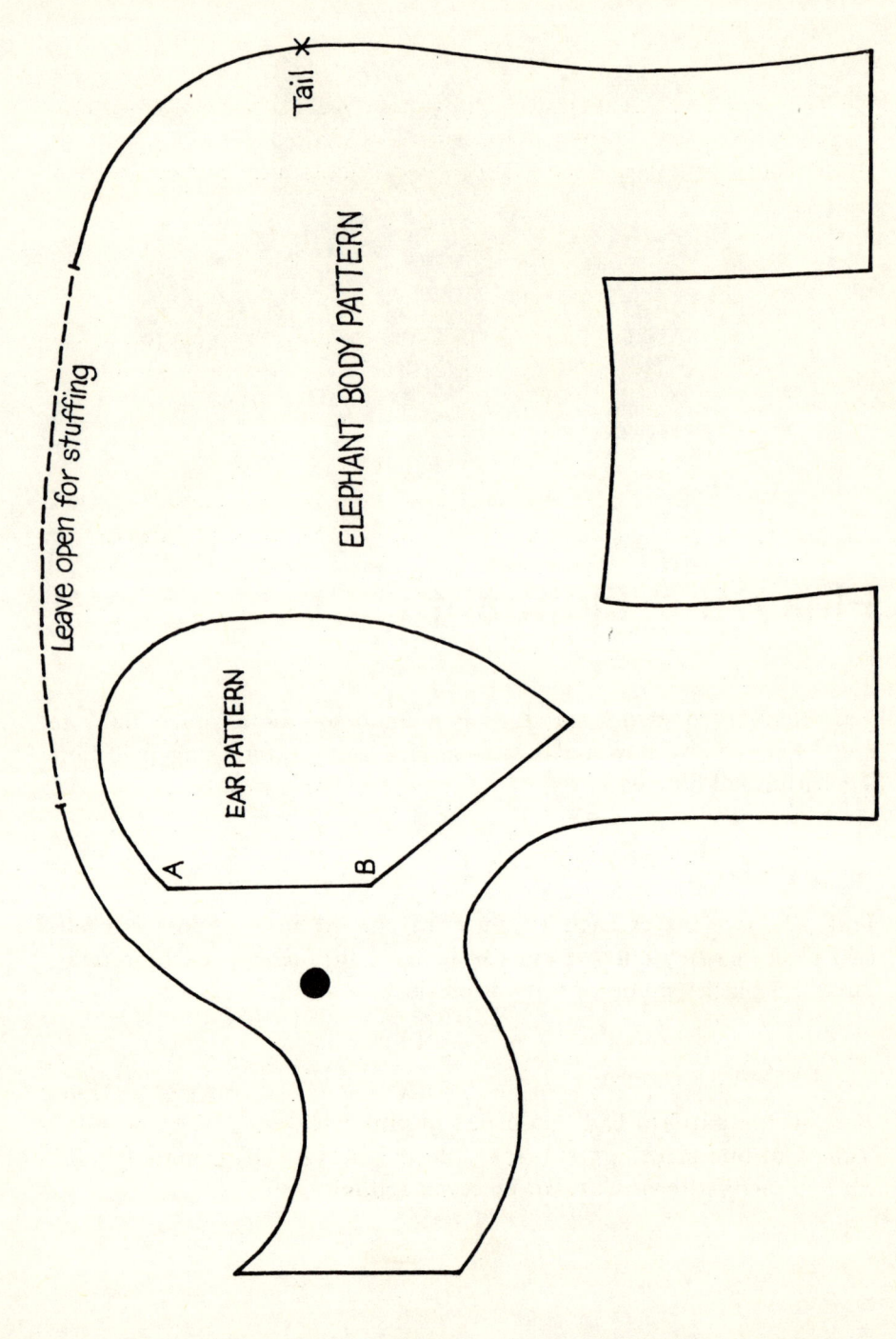

ELEPHANT BODY PATTERN

EAR PATTERN

A

B

Tail

Leave open for stuffing

Pin the two pieces together. Blanket stitch, with pink thread used double. Leave opening for stuffing at back, see position marked on pattern. Stuff trunk, legs, then body. Use thread double and blanket stitch to close opening.

EARS

Sew one to each side of head. See position on pattern. Use pink thread double and ladder stitch twice round AB. Rest of ear flaps loose.

EYES

 Black thread, used double. Satin stitch eye on each side of head. Do vertical stitches, see diagram, as with horizontal stitches the trunk obstructs the needle.

TAIL

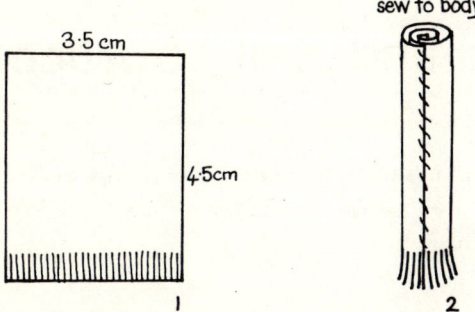

3·5 cm

4·5cm

sew to body

1   2

Cut one short end of tail into fringe, cutting about 1 cm ($\frac{1}{2}$ in) deep (Fig. 1). Roll tail and oversew to hold down end of felt (Fig. 2). Place tail on body, see position on body pattern, with stitching on underside. Using thread double, ladder stitch end of tail to body, going round twice, and holding tail pointing downwards.

Freddy Fir and Sally Spruce

Freddy Fir is easier to make as his body is sewn and stuffed in one stage. Sally Spruce is also an easy toy but is sewn and stuffed in three stages, due to her narrow branches.

MATERIALS

Freddy Fir. Emerald green felt, 33 cm × 20 cm (13 in × 8 in), or two pieces, each 20 cm (10 in) square; orange felt, two pieces, each 7 cm (2¾ in) square, and scraps of white felt; *thread*, machine twist, emerald green, orange, brown and white; stranded cotton, red; kapok or soft cotton flock.

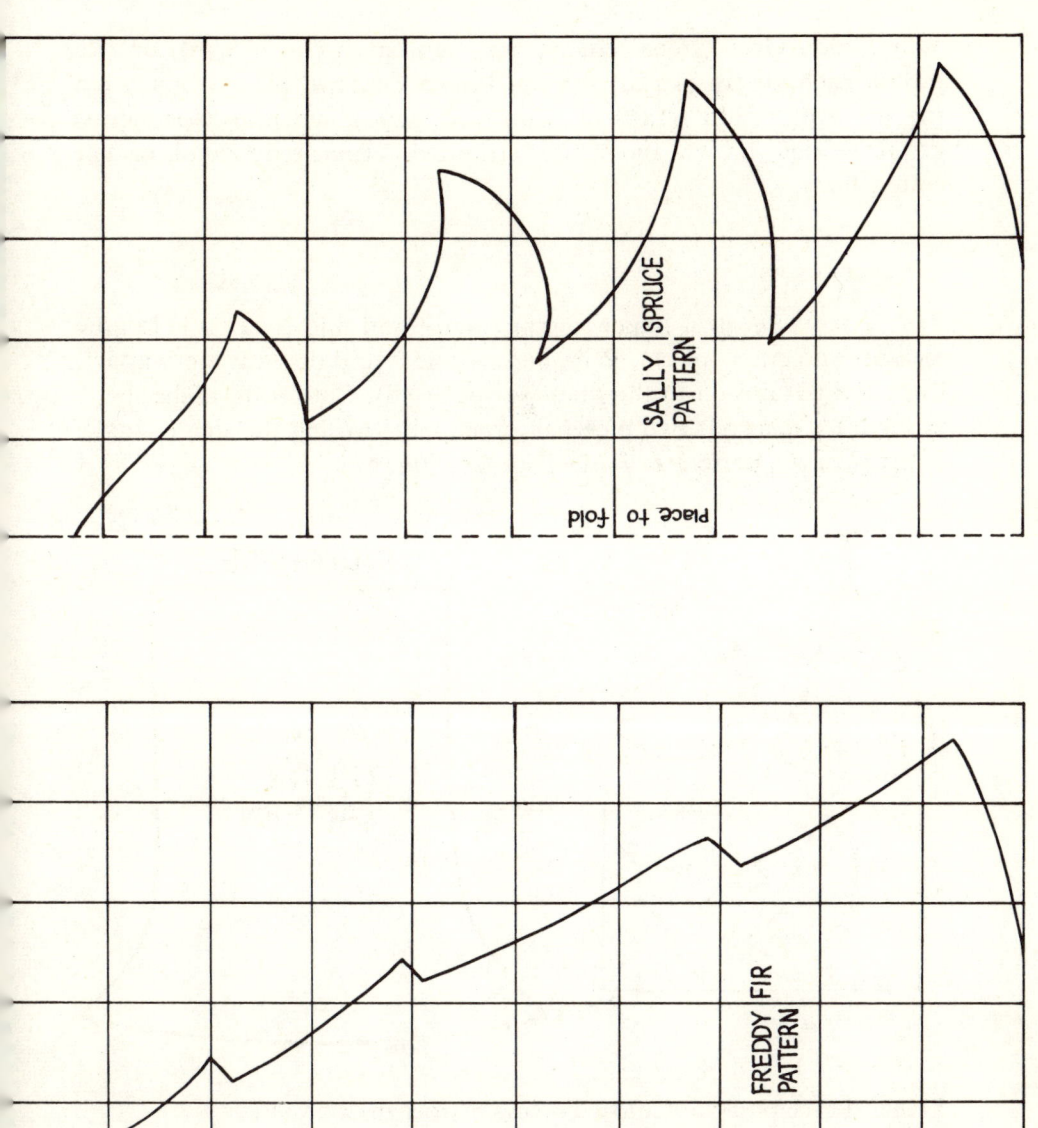

SALLY SPRUCE
PATTERN

Place to fold

FREDDY FIR
PATTERN

Place to fold

Sally Spruce. Grass green felt, 35 cm × 20 cm (14 in × 8 in), or two pieces, each 20 cm (10 in) square, brown felt, two pieces each 7 cm (2¾ in) square and scraps of white felt; *thread*, machine twist, grass green, orange, brown and white; stranded cotton, red; kapok or soft cotton flock.

PATTERN

Tree. Take a sheet of paper 20 cm square and fold it in half. It now measures 20 cm × 10 cm. Rule lines across it and down it 2 cm apart. Copy the pattern on to the lines (see page 18). Cut out to make shape as Figure 1. Cut out two pieces in green felt. If using the single length of felt turn the pattern to make it fit (see Fig. 2).

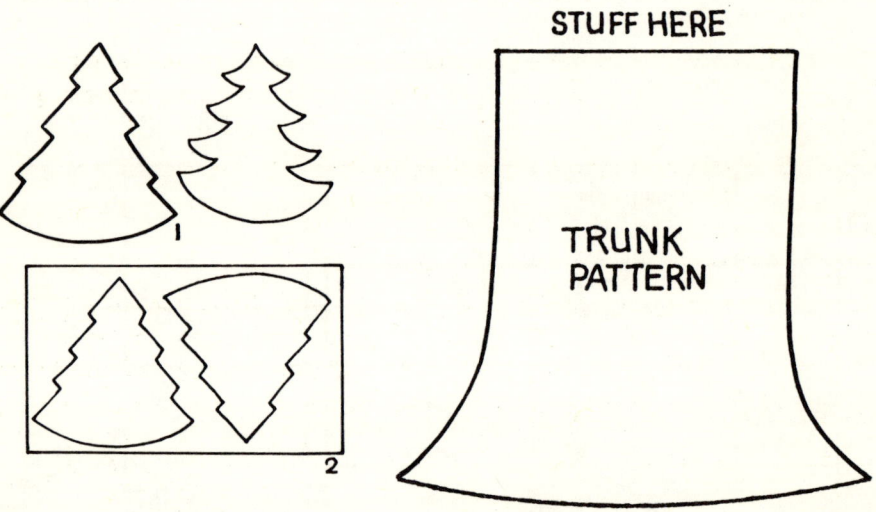

Trunk. Trace pattern. Cut two pieces in orange or brown.

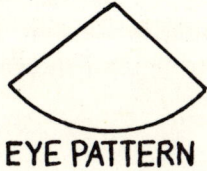

EYE PATTERN

FREDDY FIR OR SALLY SPRUCE

Eyes. Trace eye pattern. Cut two in white felt. Embroider satin stitch circle in corners with brown machine twist used double. Take a few stitches to form centre of eye, with orange machine twist used single. Just stitch through the brown—it is not necessary to go right through the eye. Place eyes on one green body. Use white thread to slipstitch round edge of eye.

Eyebrows. Brown machine twist, stem stitch, sew along them twice.

Mouth. Red stranded cotton, 3 or 4 strands, stem stitch, sew along it twice.

Nose. Red stranded cotton, two little straight stitches.

TRUNK

Pin the two trunks together. Stab-stitch, along the sides and bottom, 3 mm ($\frac{1}{8}$ in) from edge, with orange thread for Freddy Fir, or brown thread for Sally Spruce, used double. Stuff through the top and leave it open.

TREE

Pin two trees together, right sides to outside. Pin sides. Slip top of trunk between the green trees into centre of base for just over 1 cm ($\frac{1}{2}$ in). See Fig. 3 with top of trunk shaded. Pin firmly.

25

FREDDY FIR

Stab-stitch 3mm ($\frac{1}{8}$ in) from edge, with green thread used double. Sew right round green part, leaving opening for stuffing in one side (see Fig. 3). When crossing trunk, stitch through all thicknesses. Stuff tree and stab-stitch to close opening.

SALLY SPRUCE

Stab-stitch 3 mm ($\frac{1}{8}$ in) from edge, with green thread used double. Stitch round lower two branches on each side and across foot (see Fig. 4). When crossing trunk, stitch through all thicknesses. Stuff this section. Stab-stitch the next branch on each side (see Fig. 5), and stuff this section. Stab-stitch round top, leaving an opening in one side (see Fig. 6). Stuff and stab-stitch across opening.

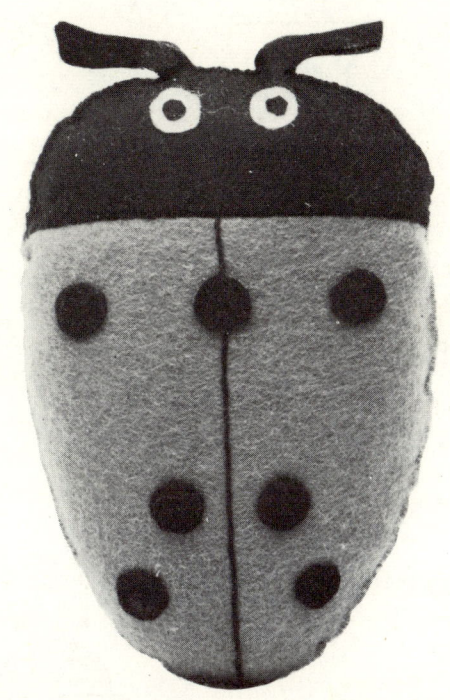

Lindy the Ladybird

Red felt, two pieces each 14 cm (5½ in) square; black felt, two pieces each 13 cm × 7 cm (5 in × 2¾ in); yellow felt, scraps for eyes; *thread*, machine twist, black and red; kapok or soft cotton flock; Copydex adhesive.

PATTERN

Body. Trace pattern on to folded paper. Cut out to make shape as

27

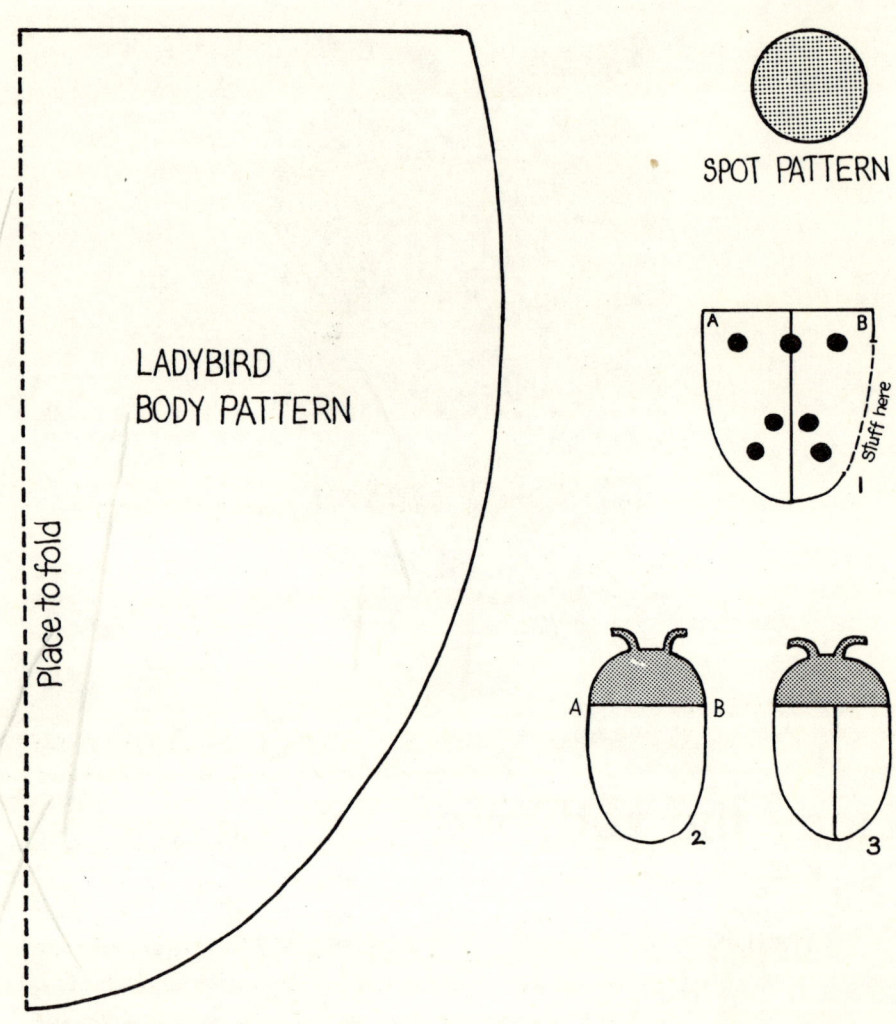

SPOT PATTERN

LADYBIRD
BODY PATTERN

Place to fold

Figure 1. Cut two in red felt.

Head, Eyes, Spots. Trace patterns. In black felt, cut two heads, seven spots and two tiny circles to be centres of eyes. In yellow felt, cut two circles for eyes.

A HEAD PATTERN B

BODY

Pin one black head on one red body. Match points A and B. Back-stitch, 6 mm ($\frac{1}{4}$ in) from edge, with black thread used double (see Fig. 2). Repeat with the other two pieces.

Draw a pencil line along the centre back of one red body on the right side. Embroider this line with stem stitch, using the black thread double (Fig. 3). This will be the upper side of the toy.

Place the two sides together, with right sides to outside. Oversew edges, with thread used double, red on body and black on head. Do not sew round the feelers. Leave opening for stuffing in one side. See position marked on Figure 1. Stuff and oversew to close opening.

FEELERS

Put a little Copydex on one pair of feelers and press the other pair on top.

SPOTS

Use a little Copydex to stick the spots on the back. Arrange them as shown on Figure 1 (page 28).

EYES

Paste with Copydex, or sew, the tiny black circles to the centre of the yellow eye circles. Paste the yellow circles to the head, just below the feelers, as shown on head pattern.

VARIATIONS

1. You could cut the head pattern without the feelers. It would still look like a ladybird without them.
2. If you do not like sewing with black thread on black felt round the head, when it may be difficult to see the stitches, sew with red all the way round.

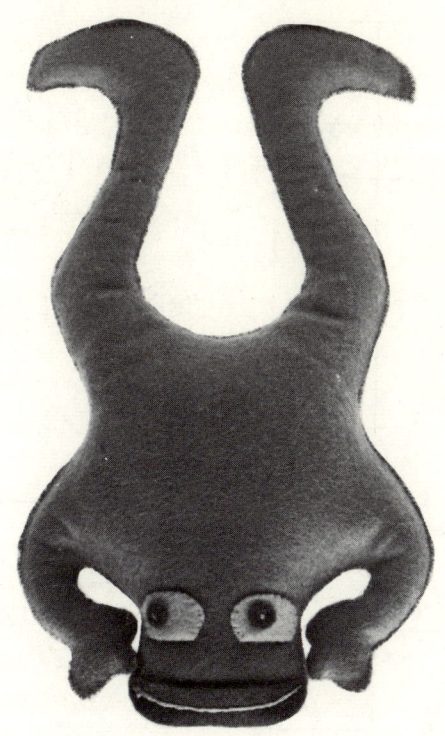

Leapy Frog

Grass green felt, two pieces each 22 cm × 16 cm (8¾ in × 6¼ in); scraps of orange and emerald green felt; *thread*, machine twist, grass green and orange; kapok or soft cotton flock.

PATTERN

Body. Take a piece of paper 22 cm × 16 cm and fold it in half. It now

31

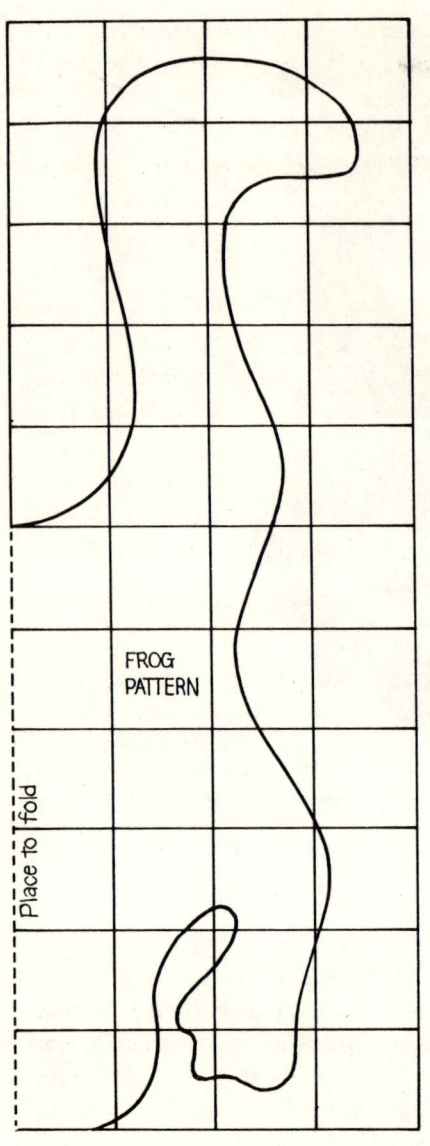

FROG
PATTERN

Place to fold

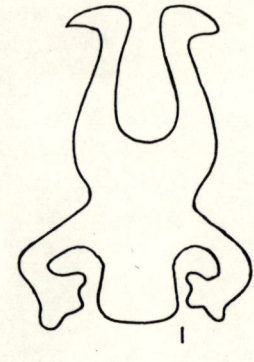

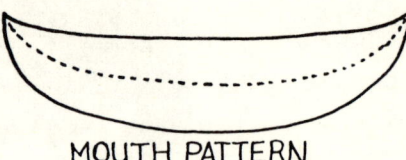

MOUTH PATTERN

EYE PATTERN

measures 22 cm × 8 cm. Rule lines across it and down it 2 cm apart. Copy the pattern on to these lines (see page 18). Cut out to make shape as Figure 1. Cut two pieces in grass green felt.

Mouth. Trace pattern. Cut one in emerald green felt.

Eyes. Trace pattern. Cut two pieces full size in orange felt and two circles in emerald green felt.

FEATURES

Mouth. Place on one of the body pieces (see Fig. 2). Use orange thread and stem stitch a line along centre of mouth. This is shown dotted on mouth pattern. Take the stitches through mouth and body and sew along two or three times.

Eyes. Place green circle to one end of each orange eye. Use orange thread and stitch together through centre of green circle to form dot in middle of eye. Place eyes on head. Use orange thread to slipstitch round edge of eye.

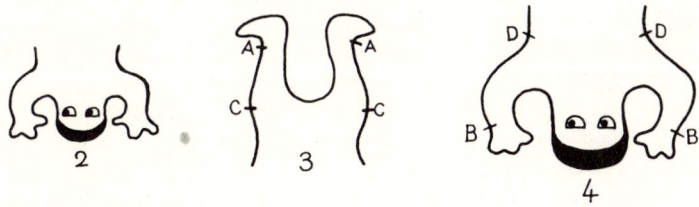

FROG

Pin two frogs together, right sides to outside. Oversew edges, with grass green thread used double. Sew from A to A round the legs (see Fig. 3). Then sew from B to B round the head (Fig. 4). At mouth sew only the two grass green body bits. It looks neater if stitches do not go through the darker green mouth.

A stuffing stick makes the narrow limbs easy to stuff.

Stuff one back foot. Sew from A to C (see Fig. 3). Stuff this leg. Repeat with other back foot and leg.

Stuff one front foot. Sew from B to D (Fig. 4). Stuff this leg. Repeat with other front foot and leg.

Sew remainder of one side. Stuff head and body through the other side then sew it.

Flutter-by the Butterfly

The butterfly is a novelty mascot, not intended for babies or toddlers. It has a pipe-cleaner on its back so that it can be hung up or clipped over an article, such as a dressing-table mirror. If it is wanted for a baby, make it without the pipe-cleaner, or sew on a brass curtain ring so that it can be hung up.

MATERIALS

Yellow felt, two pieces each 20 cm × 17 cm (8 in × 6½ in); orange felt, scraps and one piece, 10 cm × 3 cm (4 in × 1¼ in); scraps of black felt; *thread*, machine twist, yellow; kapok or soft cotton flock; Copydex adhesive; a pipe-cleaner, yellow if possible; black ballpen.

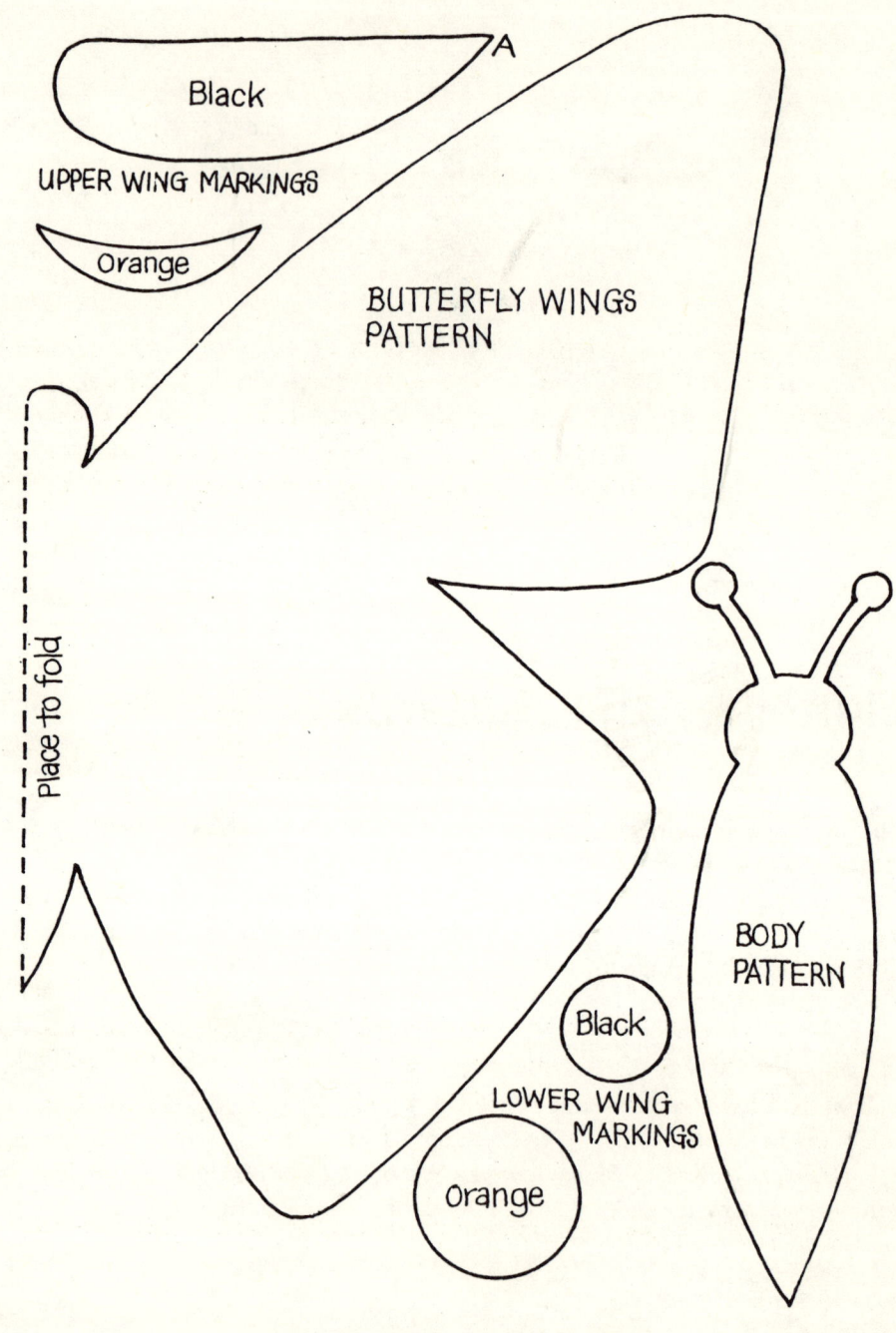

Black

UPPER WING MARKINGS

Orange

BUTTERFLY WINGS
PATTERN

Place to fold

A

BODY
PATTERN

Black

LOWER WING
MARKINGS

Orange

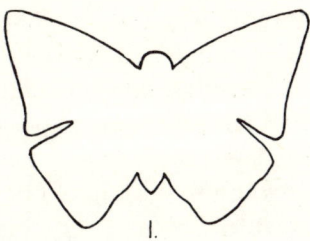

1.

Trace pattern for wings. Lay it on a piece of folded paper and cut out to make a shape like Figure 1. Cut two pieces in yellow felt. Trace rest of patterns. Orange felt; cut two upper wing markings, two lower wing markings and one body. Black felt; cut two upper wing markings and two lower wing markings. If it is too tricky to cut the antennae the butterfly looks quite effective without them.

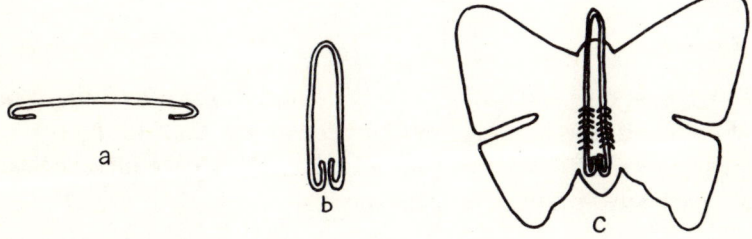

PIPE-CLEANER

(a) Bend over each end to lose sharp points.

(b) Fold cleaner in half.

(c) Use yellow thread double to sew ends of cleaner firmly to back of one butterfly. Place ends near base of body. Safest method is to sew across one cleaner and then across the other, putting the needle between the cleaners each time.

WINGS

Pin the two sides together, pipe-cleaner to outside. Blanket stitch (oversew or stab-stitch if preferred) wings using yellow thread double. Sew right round leaving two openings for stuffing on upper wings. See dotted lines on Figure 2. Through one opening stuff lower wing and upper wing. Blanket stitch across opening to close it. Through other opening stuff central body, lower wing and upper wing, then sew across opening. Do not try to put stuffing into tip of tail and head. It would be tricky and they do not need it.

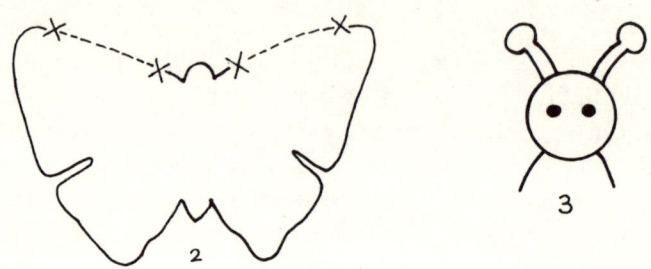

BODY

Mark two eyes on head with black ballpen. Also mark a line round the foot of the head (see Fig. 3). Put Copydex on the back of the body. Now stick it to the centre front of the butterfly. Press carefully at head and tail to make sure it sticks at these points.

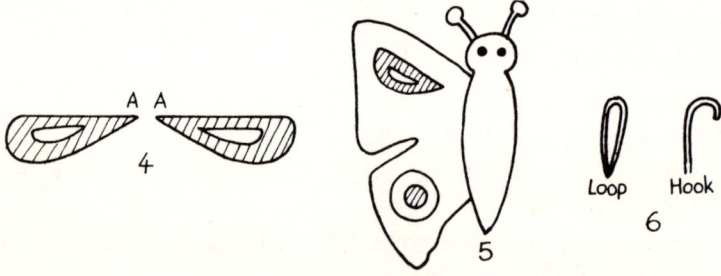

Use Copydex to stick all these bits.

Upper wings. Stick orange marking to black marking. Lay as **Figure** 4 to make a pair as narrow point A is to be nearest body. Stick black to upper wings (Fig. 5).

Lower wings. Stick black circle to orange circle. Stick orange to lower wings (Fig. 5).

The pipe-cleaner can be left as a loop or can be turned over at the top to form a hook (Fig. 6).

Sea Horse

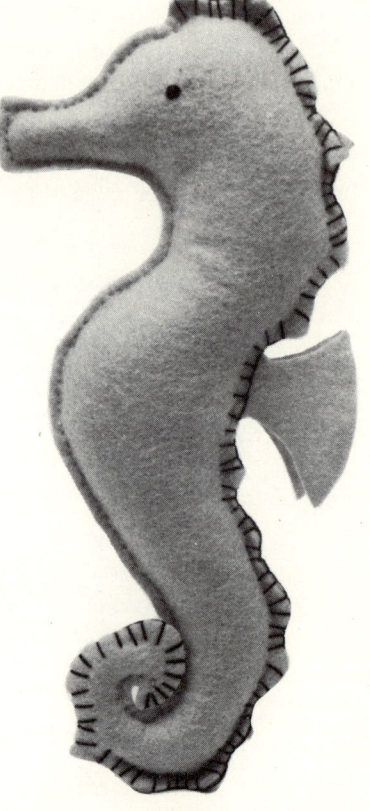

MATERIALS

Orange felt, two pieces each 26 cm × 12 cm (10½ in × 4¾ in); *thread*, machine twist, orange and black; kapok or soft cotton flock.

PATTERN

Take a sheet of paper 26 cm × 12 cm. Rule lines across it and down it 2 cm apart. Copy the pattern on to these lines (see page 18). Cut out. Cut two pieces in orange felt.

ASSEMBLY

Pin the two pieces together. Blanket stitch, with black thread used double, right down the back, from A to B (see lines on pattern). The two fins at centre back remain unsewn. When passing them keep doing blanket stitch through both thicknesses of body from C to D.

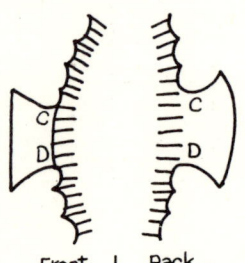

Front I. Back

The front of the toy will show correct blanket stitch, but the back will only show straight stitches (see Fig. 1). When sewing is finished return to back of fin and take a few straight stitches along CD to make the sewing look like that on the front.

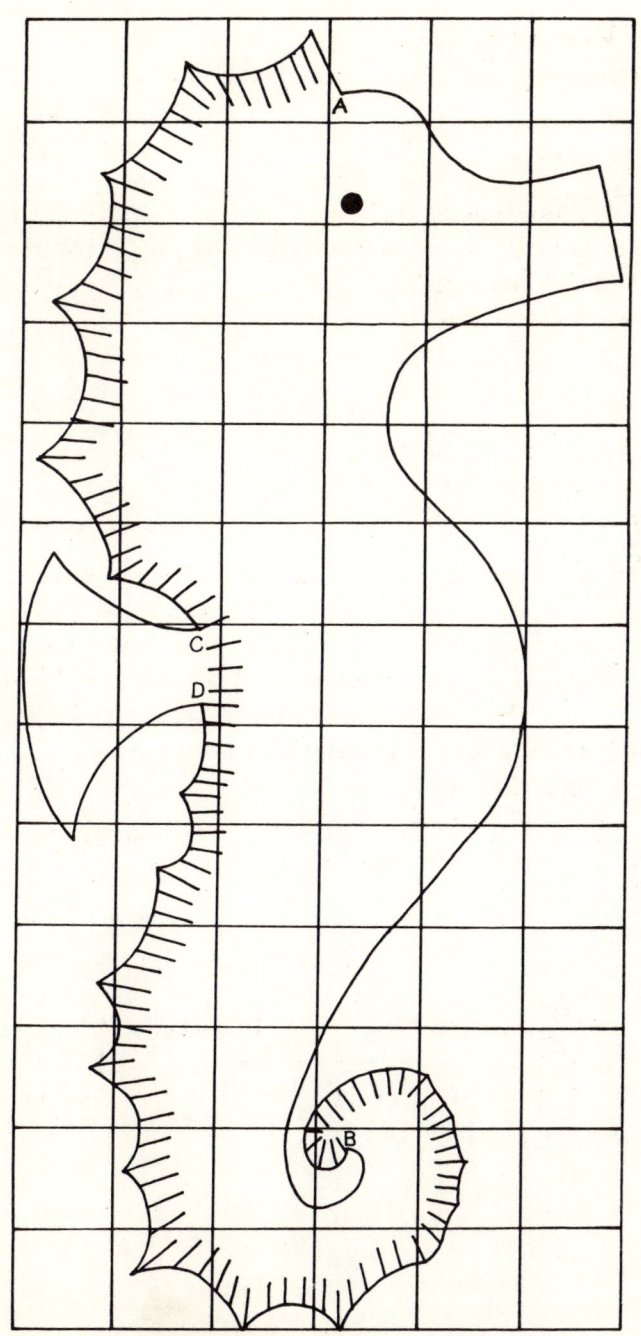

Sew one on each side of the head. Black machine twist, used double, satin stitch.

STUFFING

Front of sea horse is sewn with stab-stitch, 3 mm ($\frac{1}{8}$ in) from edge, with orange thread used double.

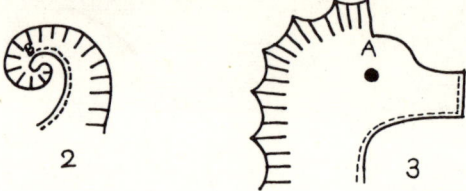

Start at B. Lay a tiny bit of stuffing in the curl of the tail for about 2·5 cm (1 in) then stab-stitch along this section (see Fig. 2). Continue like this, stuffing for about 2·5 cm (1 in) then sewing that section. Once tail is finished, change the method and sew for a few cms, and then stuff. Work up to the head. Sew round two sides of the snout (Fig. 3), then stuff before sewing along top and finishing at point A under the first black blanket stitches.

Dippy Dolphin and Dilly Dolphin

Dilly Dolphin is easier to make as she just needs one line of sewing to indicate the back. More lines can be done if desired. Dippy Dolphin has a piece of black felt sewn on top of the green body to give a dark back.

MATERIALS

Dilly Dolphin
Lime green felt, two pieces each 22 cm × 10 cm ($8\frac{3}{4}$ in × 4 in); black felt, two pieces each 6 cm × 3 cm ($2\frac{1}{2}$ in × $1\frac{1}{4}$ in); *thread*, machine twist, lime green, stranded cotton, black; kapok or soft cotton flock.

Dippy Dolphin
Lime green felt, two pieces each 22 cm × 10 cm ($8\frac{3}{4}$ in × 4 in); black felt, two pieces each 20 cm × 7 cm (8 in × $2\frac{3}{4}$ in); *thread*, machine twist, lime green, black and orange, stranded cotton, black; kapok or soft cotton flock.

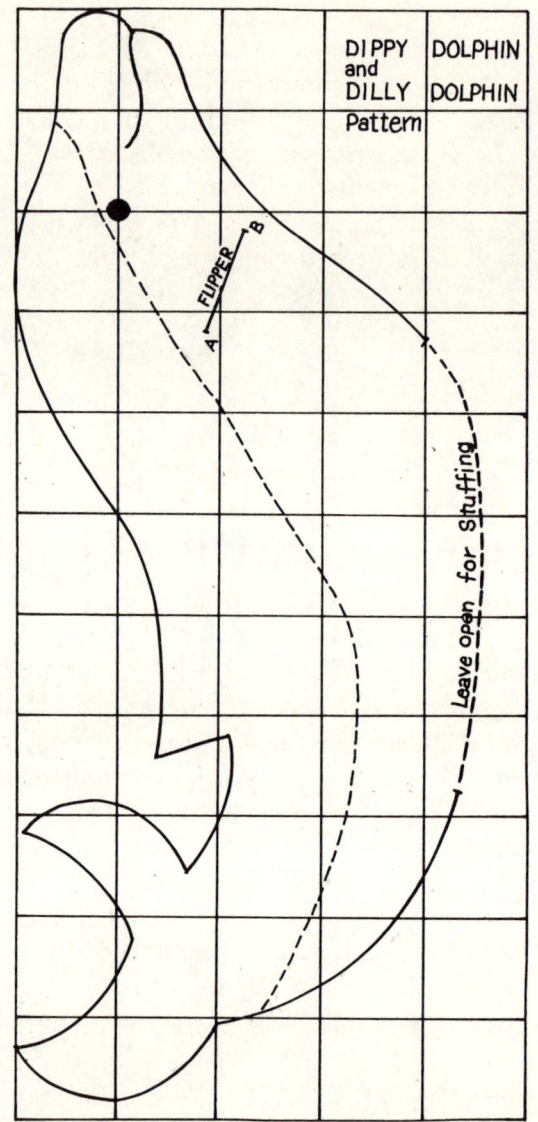

DIPPY DOLPHIN
and
DILLY DOLPHIN
Pattern

FLIPPER

A

B

Leave open for Stuffing

Body. Take a sheet of paper, 22 cm × 10 cm. Rule lines across it and down it 2 cm apart. Copy the pattern on to these lines (see page 18). Cut out. For each toy cut two pieces in lime green felt. Cut paper pattern at dotted line (or make a second pattern and cut it).
Dilly. Put aside for the moment.
Dippy. Use this upper body pattern to cut two pieces in black felt.
Flippers. Trace pattern. For each toy cut two flippers in black felt.

DILLY DOLPHIN

Upper Back. Lay pattern of upper back on one piece of green felt. Lightly pencil along edge. Pencil mark should be where dotted line is shown on main pattern. Embroider this line with black stranded cotton, 2 strands, stem stitch. Repeat on second piece of green felt but sew on other side, as shown in Figure 1, to make a pair. If desired, fill in upper back with three rows of running stitch, black stranded cotton, 1 strand, (Fig. 2). Do not sew too near edge or sewing will disappear into seam.

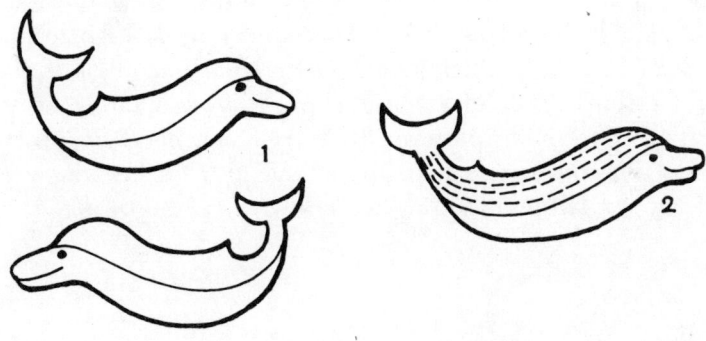

Features. Black stranded cotton, 2 strands.

Eye, satin stitch. Mouth, stem stitch. See position on pattern.

Flippers. Sew one to each side of body. Position shown on dolphin pattern. Stab-stitch twice across AB, with black thread used double. Rest of flipper stays unsewn.

Assembly. Pin the two pieces together, with right sides to outside. Stab-stitch, 3 mm ($\frac{1}{8}$ in) from edge, with green thread used double. Leave opening for stuffing, see position marked on pattern. Stuff. Stab-stitch to close opening.

DIPPY DOLPHIN

Upper Back. Pin one black back to one green dolphin side and tack it down. With orange thread used double, join the black and green together with herringbone stitch (or any decorative stitch) along the middle of the body (see Fig. 3). Repeat with second two pieces, but sew on other side, as shown in Figure 1 to make a pair.

Features and Flippers. As Dilly Dolphin.

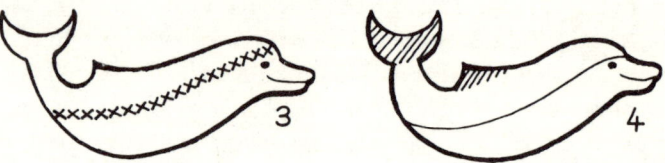

Assembly. Pin the two pieces together, with right sides to outside. Oversew, with black thread used double, round outside of black portion, sewing through all four thicknesses of felt. With lime green thread used double, oversew outside of green portion, leaving opening for stuffing. See position marked on pattern. Stuff. It is not necessary to stuff the shaded portions on Figure 4. As these have four thicknesses of felt they are stiff enough without stuffing. Oversew to close opening.

Polly Parrot

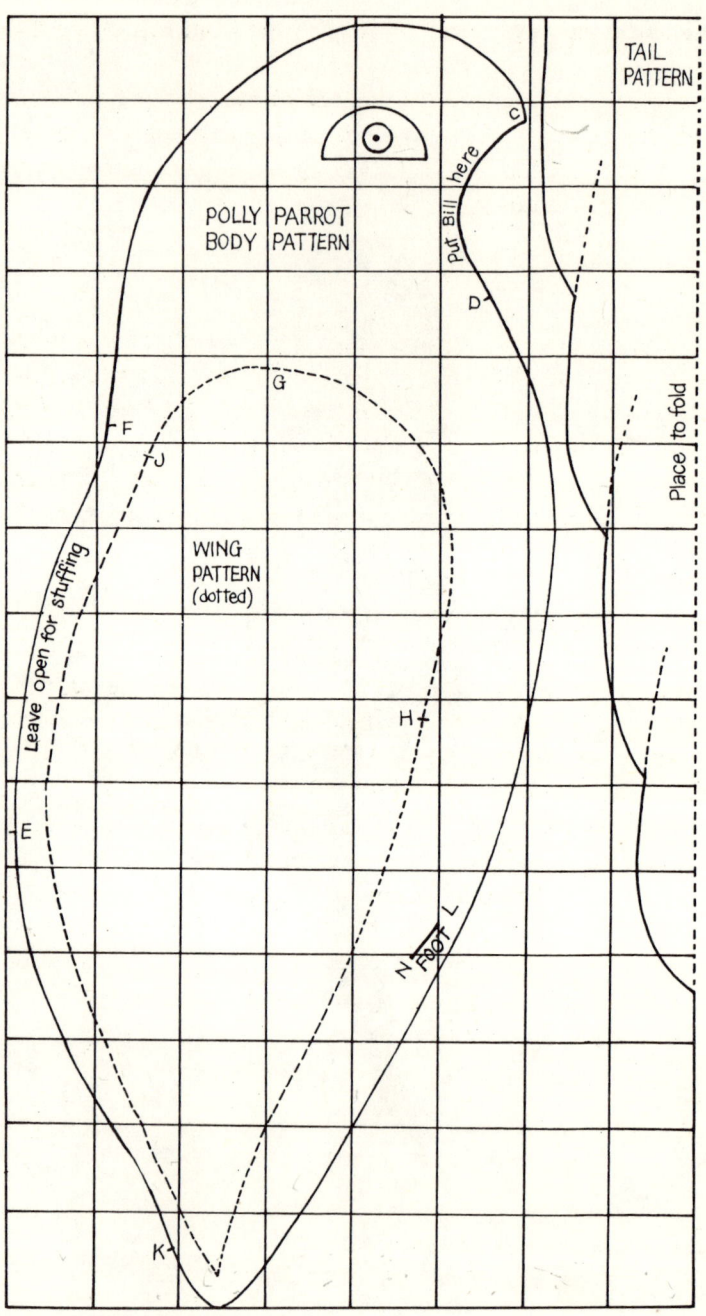

TAIL
PATTERN

POLLY PARROT
BODY PATTERN

Put Bill here

C

D

Place to fold

G

F

J

WING
PATTERN
(dotted)

Leave open for stuffing

H

E

N FOOT L

K

The parrot measures just over 45 cm (18 in) from top of head to tip of tail.

It can use up odd pieces of brightly coloured felts as body, wings and tail can all be different. Choose from red, emerald green, grass green, royal blue, light blue and yellow. Original had red body, grass green wings and royal blue tail.

MATERIALS

Felt for body, two pieces each 30 cm × 13 cm (12½ in × 5 in); felt for wings, two pieces each 22 cm × 10 cm (8½ in × 4 in); felt for tail, one piece 23 cm × 8 cm (9 in × 3 in); yellow felt for bill and feet, one piece 14 cm (5½ in) square or six small pieces; white and black felt for eyes; *thread*, machine twist, yellow, white and colours to match body, wings and tail; kapok or soft cotton flock; 2 pipe-cleaners, each 12 cm (4¾ in) long.

PATTERN

Body. Take a sheet of paper 30 cm × 14 cm. Rule lines across it and down it 2 cm apart. Copy the pattern on to these lines (see page 18). Cut out. Cut two pieces in felt.

Wings. Copy dotted line on body pattern on to the squared paper. Cut out. Cut two pieces in felt. Make cuts round foot of wing to give feather effect (Fig. 1).

Tail. Take a sheet of paper 24 cm × 8 cm and fold it in half. It now measures 24 cm × 4 cm. Rule lines as for body. Cut out to make shape as Figure 2. Cut one piece in felt. Make cuts up each side of tail to give feather effect. See dotted lines on pattern.

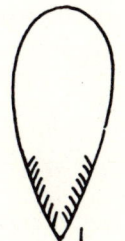
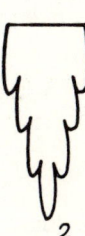

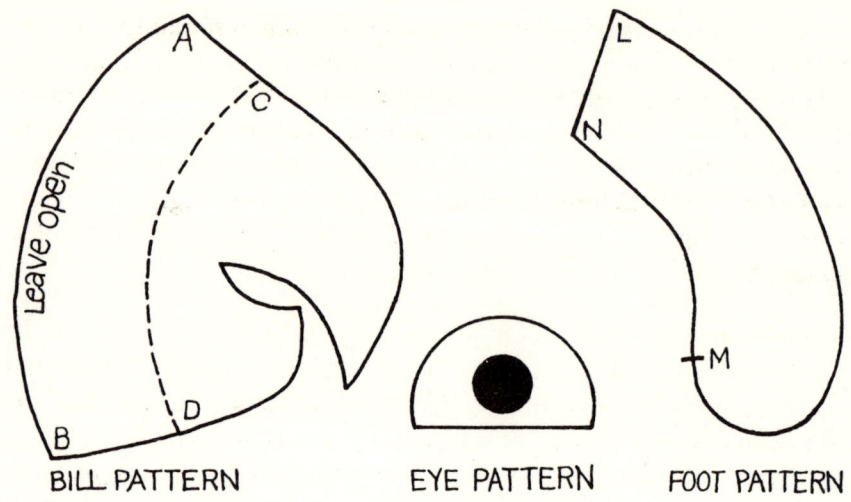

BILL PATTERN   EYE PATTERN   FOOT PATTERN

Bill, Foot, Eye. Trace patterns. Cut two bills and four feet in yellow. Cut two eye pieces full size in white and two circles for centre of eye in black.

BILL

Pin two pieces together. Stab-stitch, 3 mm ($\frac{1}{8}$ in) from edge, with yellow thread used double, from A to B going round points. Put a little stuffing into each point of bill but only going as far as dotted line CD on pattern.

EYES

Place black circle in centre of each white eye. Use yellow thread double and stitch together through centre of black circle to form dot in middle of eye.

BODY

Pin the two pieces together. Slip bill between the two body bits, matching points C and D and pin firmly. Stab-stitch bodies, 3 mm ($\frac{1}{8}$ in) from edge with thread used double, working from E round the tail and up the front to C. Work through all four thicknesses when crossing the bill. Place eye on one side of head. Use white thread to slipstitch round edge of eye. See position on body pattern. Repeat with second eye on other side of head.

Continue stab-stitching body from C to F. Stuff, beginning at tail and working up to opening, then going to head and working down to opening. Stab-stitch to close opening.

WINGS

Ladder stitch, with thread used double, top of one wing to each side of body. See position on body pattern. Most secure method is to start at G. Ladder stitch to H. Take two or three oversewing stitches to strengthen sewing. Ladder stitch back from H to J round top of wing. Take two or three oversewing stitches at J. Then ladder stitch back to G and finish off thread.

TAIL

Use thread double. Gather along top of tail. Draw up to measure 4 cm ($1\frac{1}{2}$ in). Finish off thread (Fig. 3). Pin loose ends of wings up on to body to keep them out of the way. Ladder stitch gathered end of tail firmly round top of body at point K, using thread double. Sew along twice.
Hint. Gathers usually make tail curve a little. To fit it on to curved body as it lies naturally (see Fig. 4), makes end feathers cling in awkwardly. Turn tail over so that gathers lie in what seems to be the wrong direction (Fig. 5). Sew to body and the end feathers look much better.

Turn back ends of pipe-cleaners to lose sharp points (Fig. 6). Fold each cleaner in half (Fig. 7). Pin two yellow feet together. Stab-stitch, 3 mm ($\frac{1}{8}$ in) from edge, with yellow thread used double, from L to M, going round toe. Slip in pipe-cleaner, putting curved end into toe. Finish stab-stitching to N. Place a foot on each side of body, see position on body pattern. Using yellow thread double ladder stitch twice round NL.

 7

6

Chicky Chick

MATERIALS

Yellow fur fabric, 36 cm × 18 cm with pile stroking along the 18 cm direction ($\frac{1}{4}$ yd at 54 in wide will make four chickens); orange cotton or thin woollen cloth, scraps for bill; *thread*, machine twist, yellow and orange, stranded cotton, black; kapok or soft cotton flock.

53

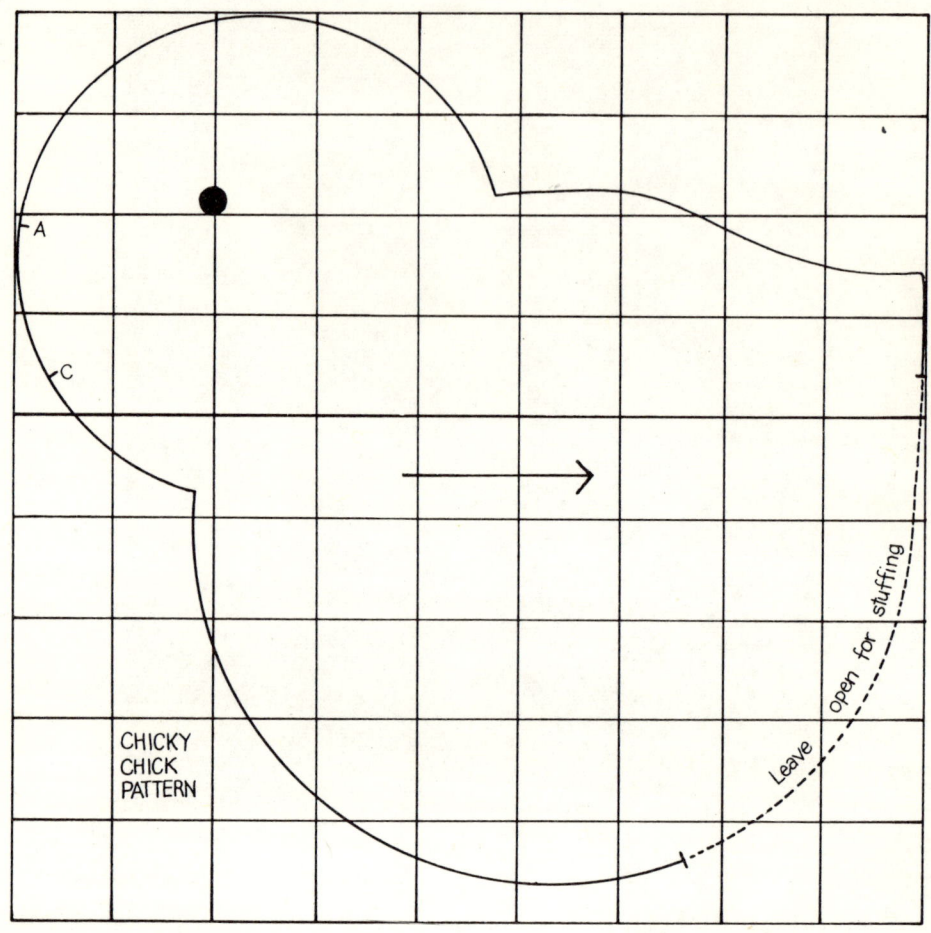

A

C

CHICKY
CHICK
PATTERN

Leave open for stuffing

PATTERN

Body. Take a sheet of paper 18 cm square: rule lines across it and down it, 2 cm apart. Copy the pattern on to these lines (see page 18). Cut out. Lay pattern on yellow fur fabric with pile stroking in direction of arrow. Cut one body, then turn pattern over and cut second body in order to make a pair (see Fig. 1).

Bill. Trace pattern. Cut two bills in orange.

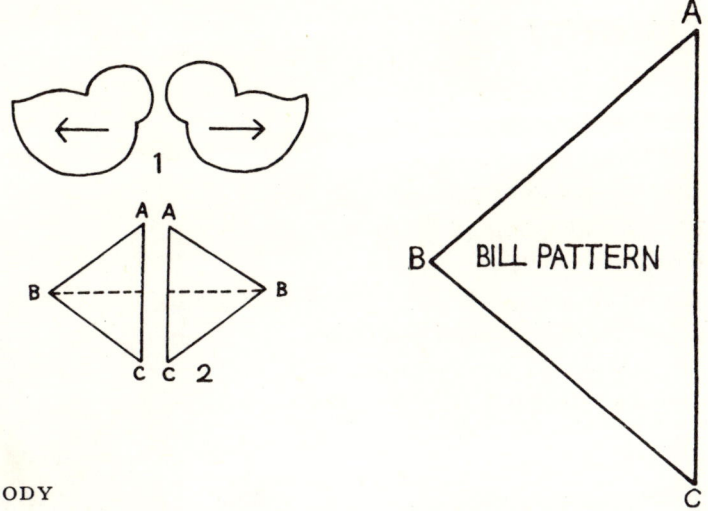

BODY

Pin the two pieces together with wrong sides to outside. Backstitch, 6 mm ($\frac{1}{4}$ in) from edge, with yellow thread used double. Leave opening for stuffing at back, see position marked on pattern. Round the opening turn edges over to wrong side and tack down. Turn to right side. Stuff. Use thread double and ladder stitch to close opening.

BILL

On right side of each bill embroider a line with black stranded cotton, using one strand only. Follow Figure 2 to make a pair. Pin the two bills together with wrong sides to outside. Backstitch, 6 mm ($\frac{1}{4}$ in) from edge, with orange thread, sewing round ABC. Turn edges round AC over to wrong side and tack down. Turn to right side. Stuff. Place on head seam, see AC on body pattern, and using orange thread double, ladder stitch twice round AC.

EYES

Black stranded cotton, 4 strands. Satin stitch eye on each side of head. See position on body pattern.

Billy Bunny

Blue woollen cloth ¼ m (¼ yd) will make three with careful cutting; white fur fabric, two pieces each 11 cm × 6 cm (4¼ in × 2¼ in) for ears, one piece 5 cm (2 in) square for tail; *thread*, machine twist, blue, white and black; kapok or soft cotton flock; ribbon 55 cm (22 in).

PATTERN

Body. Take a piece of paper 22 cm × 12 cm and fold it in half. It now measures 22 cm × 6 cm. Rule lines across it and down it 2 cm apart. Copy the pattern on to these lines (see page 18). Cut out to make shape as shown on left. Cut two pieces in blue cloth.

Ears and Tail. Trace patterns. Cut two ears in blue cloth. Cut two ears and one tail in fur fabric, laying pattern on fabric with pile stroking in direction of arrow.

BODY

Pin the two pieces together with wrong sides to outside. Backstitch, 6 mm (¼ in) from edge, with blue thread used double. Leave opening for stuffing at one side, see position marked on pattern. Round the opening turn edges over to wrong side and tack down. Turn to right side. Stuff. Use thread double and ladder stitch to close opening.

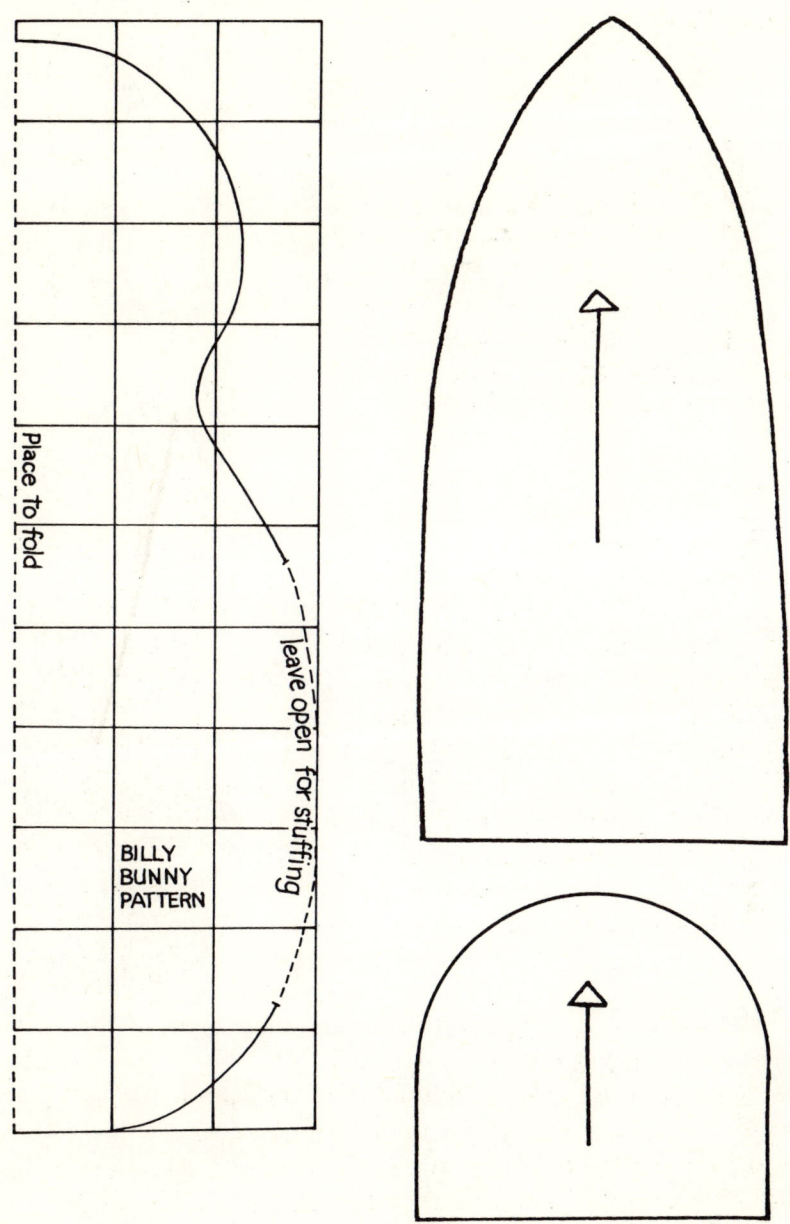

Place to fold

leave open for stuffing

BILLY
BUNNY
PATTERN

EARS

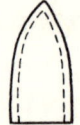  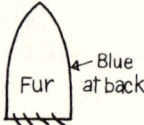

For each ear join one blue and one fur ear together, with wrong sides to outside. Backstitch, 6 mm ($\frac{1}{4}$ in) from edge along long sides.

Round foot, turn edges over to wrong side. Tack down.

Turn to right side. Take a few stitches along foot to close opening.

Turn each corner towards the middle, so that the fur is the lining, and sew it down. It will just turn over and no more but does make the ear look more lifelike.

Sew ears to head on top seam. Fur lining faces front. Using blue thread double ladder stitch round twice.

TAIL

Turn edges over to wrong side all round. Tack down.

Place on back, just over 1 cm ($\frac{1}{2}$ in) up from seam.
Using white thread ladder stitch round twice.

All done in black thread, used double.

Eyes. Satin stitch.

Nose. Satin stitch. One straight stitch to mouth.

Mouth. Stem stitch. Sew along it a few times to make it conspicuous.

RIBBON

Tie round neck, making bow at front.

Oliver Owl

MATERIALS

Brown fur fabric, $\frac{1}{4}$ m ($\frac{1}{4}$ yd); yellow fur fabric, 13 cm × 8 cm (5 in × 3 in); *thread*, machine twist, yellow, black and brown, stranded cotton, black and orange; kapok or soft cotton flock.

PATTERN

Body. Take a sheet of paper 22 cm × 16 cm and fold it in half. It now measures 22 cm × 8 cm. Rule lines across it and down it 2 cm apart.

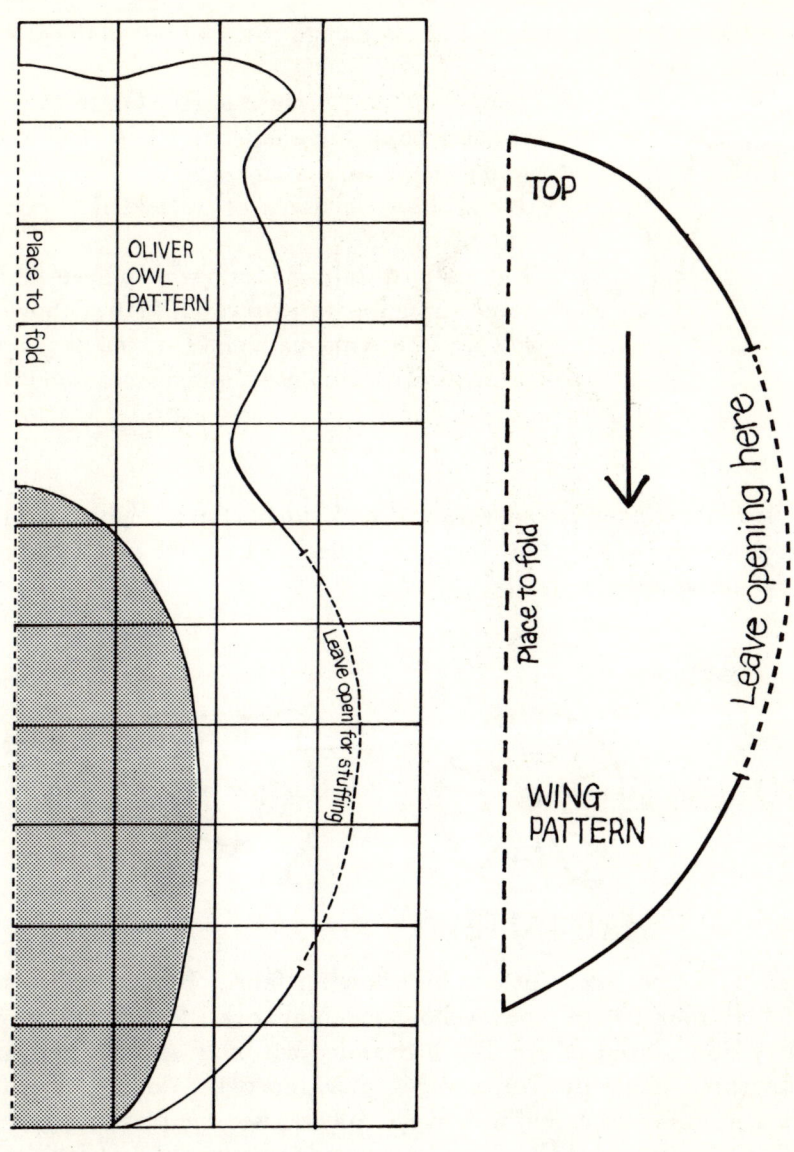

OLIVER
OWL
PATTERN

Place to fold

Leave open for stuffing

TOP

Place to fold

Leave opening here

WING
PATTERN

Copy the pattern on to these lines (see page 18). Cut out to make shape as shown below.

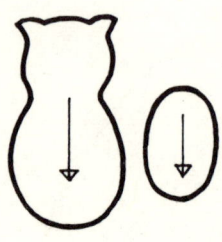

Front. Fold owl pattern again. On to the ruled squares copy the shaded portion. Cut out to make shape as shown on left.

Wings. Trace pattern on to folded paper and cut out.

Lay patterns on fur fabric with pile stroking in same direction as arrows on figures shown on left and on wing pattern. Cut out two bodies and four wings in brown and one front in yellow.

FRONT

Turn edges over to wrong side and tack down. Pin to right side of one brown body. Using yellow thread double, ladder stitch firmly to brown body, going right round.

FEATURES

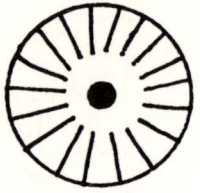

EYE PATTERN

Eyes. Trace pattern. Cut two in yellow fur fabric. Blanket stitch, small stitches, round edge with yellow machine twist to prevent fraying. Furry side is front of eye. Black stranded cotton, 6 strands, embroider satin stitch circle in centre. Black machine twist, double, take large straight stiches all round to sew eye to head, see eye pattern.

Bill. Orange stranded cotton, 6 strands. Satin stitch triangle (see above).

BODY

Pin the two pieces together, with wrong sides to outside. Backstitch, 6 mm ($\frac{1}{4}$ in) from edge with brown thread used double. Leave opening for stuffing in side, see position marked on pattern. Round the opening turned edges over to wrong sides and tack down. Turn to right side. Stuff. Use thread double and ladder stitch to close opening.

WINGS

For each wing pin two pieces together, with wrong sides to outside. Backstitch, 6 mm ($\frac{1}{4}$ in) from edge, with brown thread. Leave opening in one side, see position marked on pattern. Round the opening turn edges over to wrong side and tack down. Turn to right side. Ladder stitch to close opening.

Place one wing on each side of body. Centre top goes on side seam, just above top of yellow front. Use brown thread double and ladder stitch twice along top of wing.

Sandy Carrot

SANDY CARROT
PATTERN

Place to fold

Orange woollen cloth or cotton, two pieces each 20 cm × 16 cm (8 in × 6 in); emerald green nylon net, two strips each 30 cm × 8 cm (12 in × 3½ in); *thread*, machine twist, orange and emerald, stranded cotton, black and emerald; kapok or soft cotton flock.

PATTERN

Body. Take a piece of paper 20 cm × 16 cm and fold it in half. It now measures 20 cm × 8 cm. Rule lines across it and down it 2 cm apart. Copy the pattern on to these lines (see page 18). Cut out to make shape as Figure 1. Cut two pieces in orange.

BODY

Pin the two pieces together with wrong sides to outside. Backstitch, 6 mm (¼ in) from edge, with orange thread used double. Leave straight top open for stuffing. Round the opening turn edges on to wrong side. Using thread double, gather right round as near the top as possible. Do not pull up. Turn to right side. Stuff carrot body.

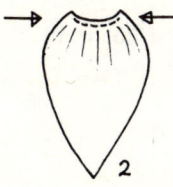

Pull up gathering thread till it is half-tight, then put more stuffing into the 'shoulders' all round the carrot (see arrows on Fig. 2). Pull up the thread tightly now and finish off gathers. There will be a small hole in centre.

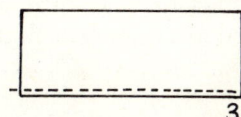

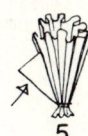

CARROT TOP

Pin the two strips of net on top of each other. Using emerald green thread single, gather along the long edge 6 mm (¼ in) from edge (see

Fig. 3). Pull up gathers as tight as possible and take two or three stitches to fix them. Then take thread through beginning of strip to pull it into a bunch (Fig. 4). Take a few stitches backwards and forwards through base of gathers to keep bunch compact. Finish off thread.

Hint. If there is a tendency for one end to stick out straight at the side (see arrow on Fig. 5), tuck it firmly into the centre of the gathered bunch. Take more stitches through the base to hold it.

ASSEMBLY

Hold the green top in the stuffing hole at top of carrot. Use the orange thread double and ladder stitch round top between carrot and net to hold them together. Keep doing this until net is held firmly and no stuffing is left showing. Finish off thread.

FEATURES

Stranded cotton, 3 strands.

Eyes. Outline outer circles in black in stem stitch. Small circle in green satin stitch. Few black stitches to make spot in centre of green.

Nose. One straight black stitch.

Mouth. Black, stem stitch.

Hint. Easiest way to place features evenly is to stick in pins for *middle* of each eye. Then embroider black circle round them. Now move pins to find sauciest position for green eyes, then sew them on that spot.

Wobbly Woo and Wobbly Winnie

This rag doll has unstuffed legs and arms and because of this it can sit easily if it is propped against a support. The legs can be crossed in a very casual manner.

It also has two faces. Woo's face on one side of the head and Winnie's on the other. It sits equally well with either face to the front.

MATERIALS

Patterned cotton, ⅓ metre, or two pieces each 40 cm × 30 cm (⅓ yd or two pieces each 16 in × 12 in); *thread*, machine twist, white; wool, thin black (or thick black thread will do); kapok or soft cotton flock.

PATTERN

Take a piece of paper, 40 cm × 32 cm and fold it in half. It now measures 40 cm × 16 cm. Rule lines across it and down it 2 cm apart. Copy the pattern on to these lines (see page 18). Cut out to make shape as Figure 1. Cut two pieces in patterned cotton.

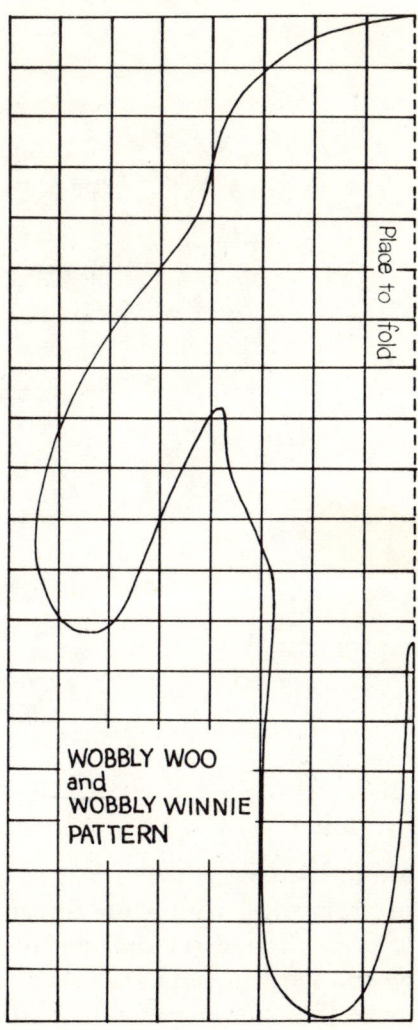

Place to fold

WOBBLY WOO
and
WOBBLY WINNIE
PATTERN

BODY

Pin the two pieces together, wrong sides to outside. Backstitch, 6 mm ($\frac{1}{4}$ in) from edge, with white thread. Leave top of head open for stuffing (Fig. 2). Round the opening turn edges over to wrong side and tack down. Turn to right side. At this stage it is worth pressing the toy to make the arms and legs flat and neat.

Backstitch across the top of the legs, so that the stuffing will not go down them. Also backstitch across the top of the arms. Slant this line

Leave open
for stuffing

2

3

from shoulder to underarm. These lines are shown dotted on Fig. 3.
Stuff the body. Use thread double and ladder stitch to close opening.

Use a wide-eyed needle with the black wool or thread. *Faintly* pencil the features first. Sew over lines twice to make them stand out. Do not worry if wisps of kapok are brought to the surface by the needle. The second lot of stitching will cover them.

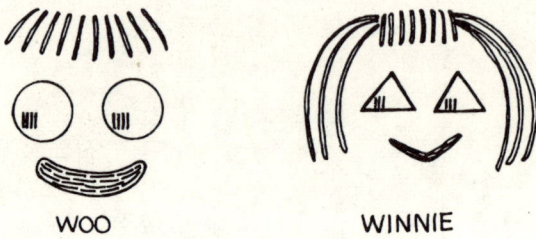

WOO   WINNIE

Hair. Stem stitch.
Eyes. Stem stitch edges. Satin stitch centres.
Mouth: Woo. Stem stitch outline. Fill it in with short straight stitches.
Mouth: Winnie. Stem stitch. Do three or four rows.

Timmy Tortoise

Patterned cotton for shell, two pieces each 22 cm × 14 cm (8¾ in × 5½ in, or ¼ yard at 36 in wide will make three tortoises); plain cotton for head, legs and tail in colour to contrast with shell, 30 cm × 22 cm (12 in × 9 in) *or* three small pieces, 9 cm × 7·5 cm (3½ in × 3 in) and eight pieces, 7·5 cm × 5 cm (3 in × 2 in); *thread*, machine twist, colours to match shell and plain cotton, stranded cotton, red and black; kapok or soft cotton flock.

PATTERN

Shell and *Tail*. Trace patterns on to folded paper. Cut out to make shapes as Figure 1. Cut two shells in patterned cotton and one tail in plain cotton.

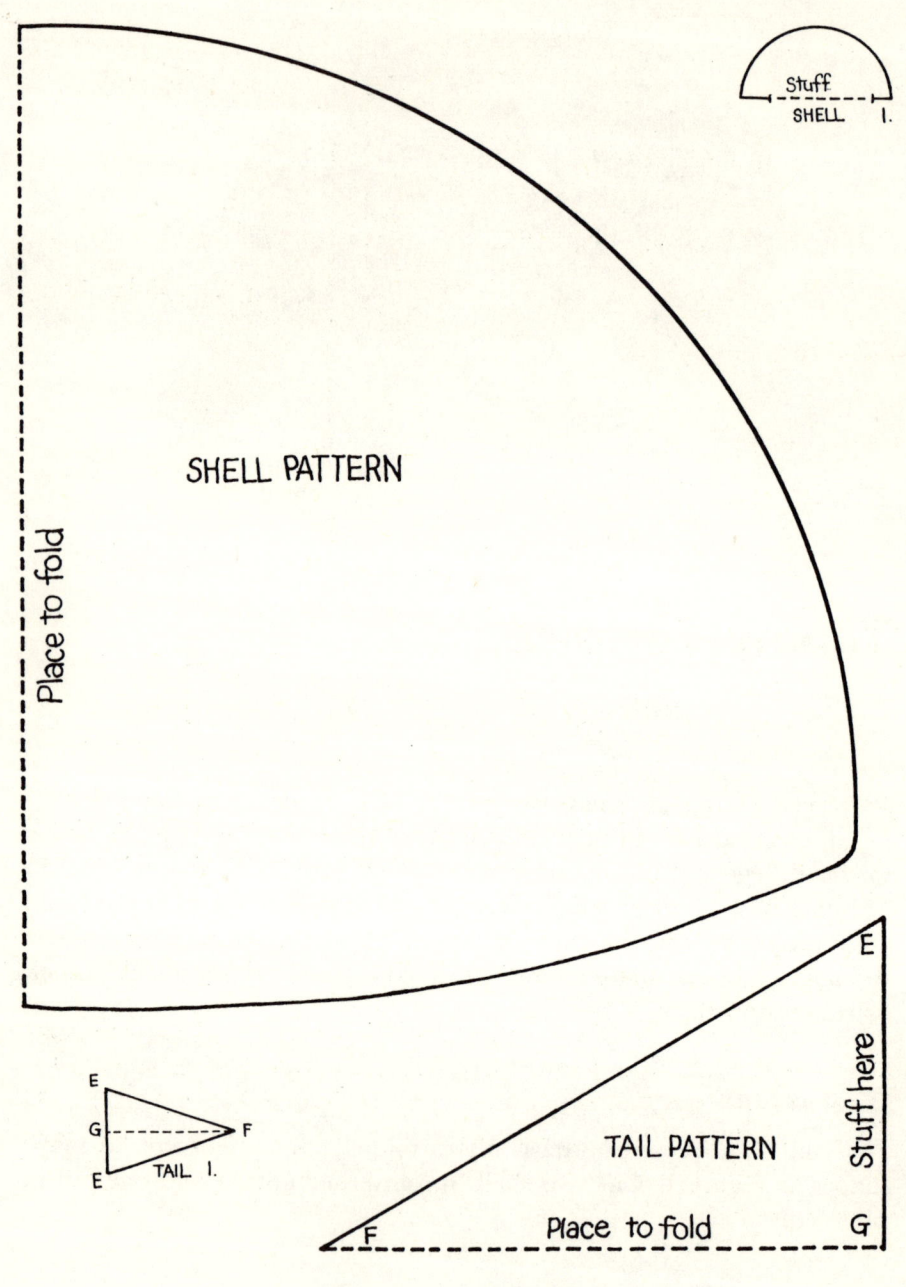

Stuff

SHELL 1.

SHELL PATTERN

Place to fold

E

G ····· F

E   TAIL 1.

E

Stuff here

TAIL PATTERN

F ····· Place to fold ····· G

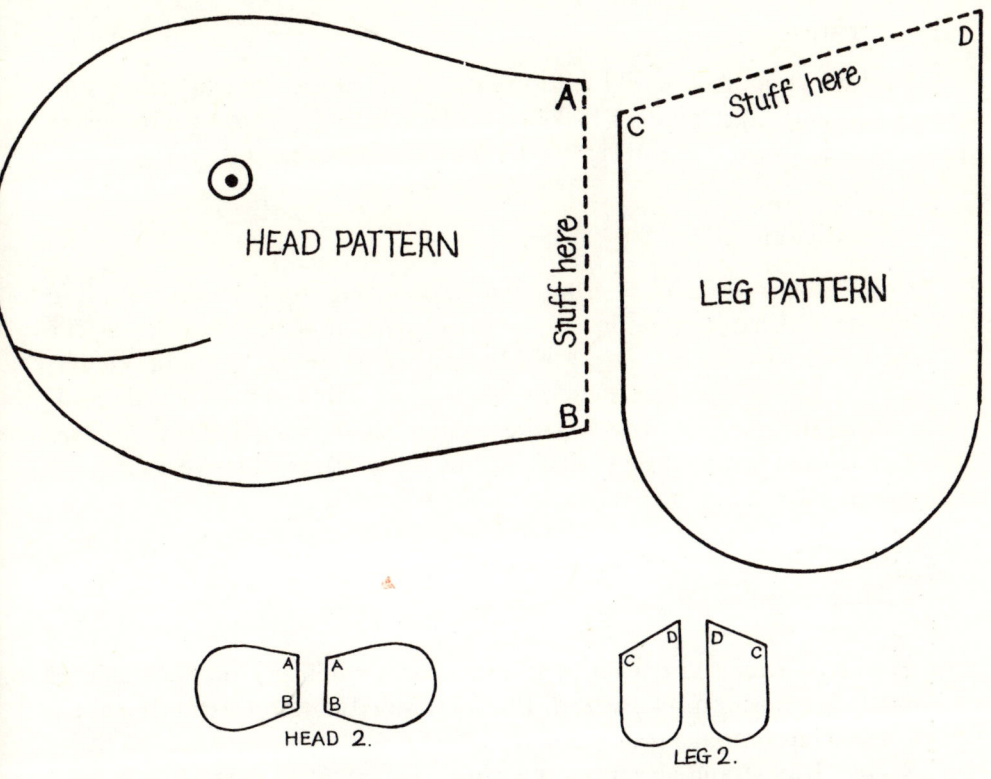

Head and *Legs*. Trace patterns. Cut two heads and eight legs in plain cotton. If cotton has a right and a wrong side turn pattern over when cutting head and legs in order to make pairs (Fig. 2).

SHELL, HEAD, LEGS

Pin two shells, two heads or two legs together, with wrong sides to outside. Backstitch, 6 mm ($\frac{1}{4}$ in) from edge. Leave opening for stuffing in base of *shell*, see position marked on Figure 1, on *head* from A to B and on *leg* from C to D. Round the opening turn edges over to wrong side and tack down. Turn to right side. Stuff. *Shell:* ladder stitch to close opening. *Head:* leave open. *Legs:* oversew to close opening.

73

TAIL

Fold tail in half along FG with wrong side to outside. Backstitch, 6 mm (¼ in) from edge along EF. Round EG turn edges over to wrong side and tack down. Turn to right side. Stuff. Leave open.

ASSEMBLY

Head. Place open neck on front seam of shell (Fig. 3). Push extra stuffing into neck at join to hold it firm and circular. Use thread double, ladder stitch twice round AB. Head will be lying straight out, probably touching the ground. Take a new double thread. Tilt head up a little and, holding it there, do a row of ladder stitch between head and shell from X, half-way up one side of neck, across top to X on other side (Fig. 4). This pulls head up and makes it look livelier (Fig. 5).

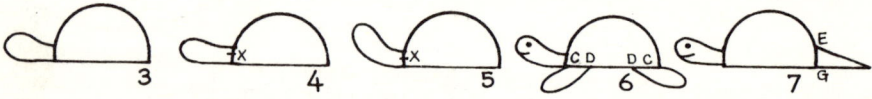

Eyes. Red stranded cotton, 3 strands. Satin stitch eye on each side of head. See position on pattern. Black stranded cotton 2 strands, take a few stitches to make spot in centre of eye.

Mouth. Red stranded cotton, 3 strands, sew along it twice.

Legs. Place legs on sides of body so that they lie along the ground. On front legs, put point C to front of shell. On back legs, put point C to back of shell (Fig. 6). Use thread double and ladder stitch twice round CD. When all four legs are sewn the body should be raised a little bit off the ground.

Tail. Place on back of shell with G at base (Fig. 7). Use thread double and ladder stitch twice around EG.

Piggy Porker

MATERIALS

Fine orange woollen cloth, 80 cm × 16 cm (32 in × 6 in); royal blue cotton, two pieces each 10 cm (4 in) square; *thread*, machine twist, orange, stranded cotton, blue and black; kapok or soft cotton flock; 1 pipe-cleaner.

PATTERN

Body. Take a sheet of paper, 26 cm × 16 cm. Rule lines across it and down it 2 cm apart. Copy the pattern on to these lines (see page 18). Cut out. Cut two pieces in orange.

Ears. Trace pattern. Cut two pieces in orange and two pieces in royal blue.

Legs. Cut four pieces in orange, each 7 cm × 4 cm (2¾ in × 1½ in).

Tail. Cut one piece in orange, 10 cm × 4 cm (4 in × 1½ in).

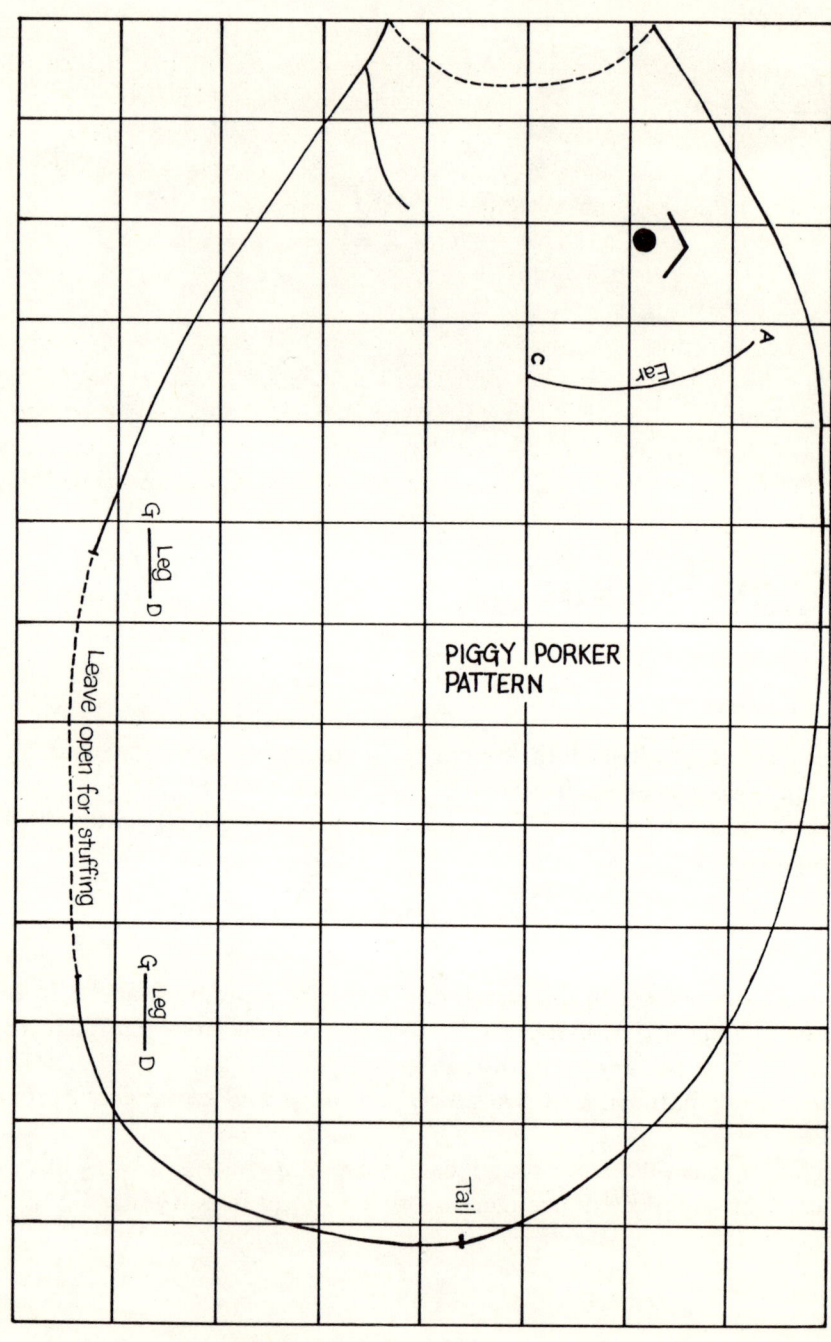

PIGGY PORKER
PATTERN

Ear

Leg

Leave open for stuffing

Leg

Tail

BODY

Pin the two pieces together, with wrong sides to outside. Backstitch, 6 mm (¼ in) from edge, with orange thread used double. Leave opening for stuffing, see position marked on pattern. Round the opening turn edges over to wrong side and tack down. Turn to right side. Stuff. Use thread double and ladder stitch to close opening.

EARS

For each ear place one orange cloth and one blue cotton piece together, with wrong sides to outside. Backstitch, 6 mm (¼ in) from edge, along the two sides, AB and BC, with orange thread. Round AC turn edges over to wrong side and tack down. Turn to right side. Take a few stitches along AC to close the opening. Use orange thread double and

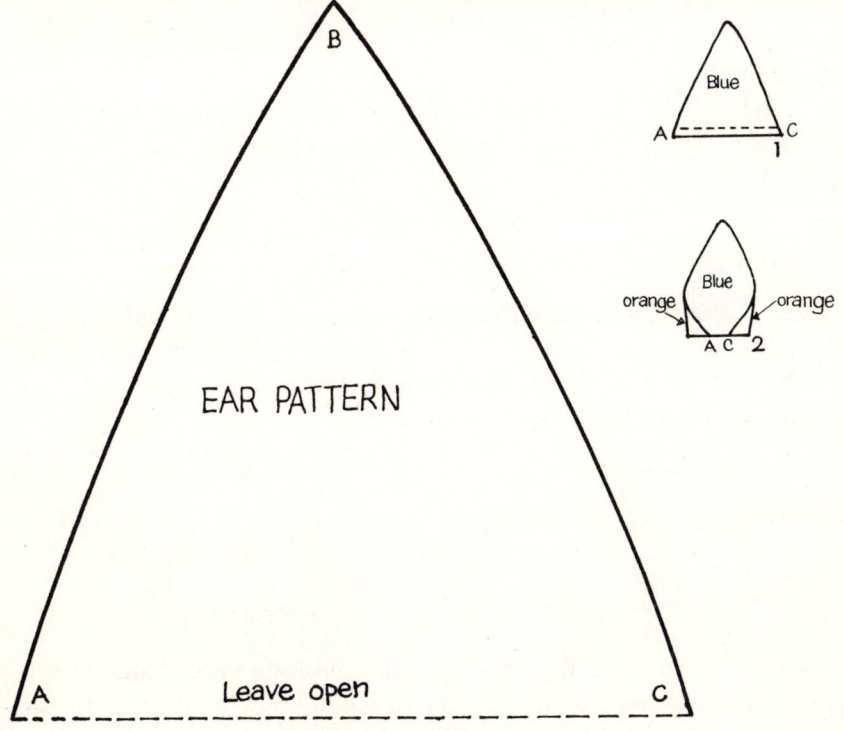

EAR PATTERN

Leave open

77

gather along AC, working close to edge on blue side (Fig. 1). It is not necessary to take stitches right through orange cloth. Draw gathers up just enough to pull ear into curved shape (Fig. 2). Fasten off thread.

Pin one ear to each side of head, blue side facing to snout. See position on body pattern. (*Hint:* Put in pins for eyes. It helps to judge if ears look correct.) Using orange thread double, ladder stitch round AC. Now tilt ear to lie forwards towards eye and ladder stitch round AC a second time.

FEATURES

All done in stranded cotton, 3 strands. Position shown on pattern.

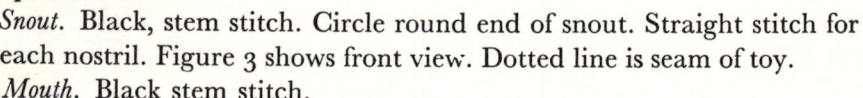

Eyes. Blue, satin stitch. A few black stitches to make spot in centre of eye.

Eyebrows. Black. Straight stitches forming a V-shape upside down.

Snout. Black, stem stitch. Circle round end of snout. Straight stitch for each nostril. Figure 3 shows front view. Dotted line is seam of toy.

Mouth. Black stem stitch.

LEGS

For each leg use one orange cloth piece (Fig. 4). Fold in half (Fig. 5), with wrong side to outside. Backstitch, 6 mm ($\frac{1}{4}$ in) from edge along DEF. Round DG turn edges over to wrong side and tack down. Turn to right side. Stuff. Leave open.

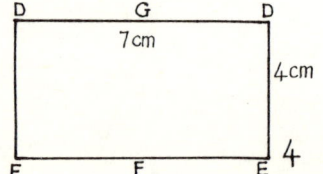
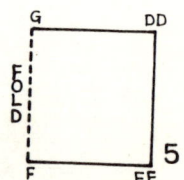

Sew two legs to each side of the body. See position marked on pattern. Easiest way is to hold pig upside down while sewing legs. Use thread double and ladder stitch twice round GD.

Bracing Legs. To make toy stand steadily brace each leg. With toy still upside down hold leg in a straight upright position. Now with thread used single do an extra row of ladder stitch between inside of leg and body to keep leg in this position.

TAIL

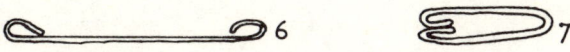

Turn back ends of pipe-cleaner to lose sharp points (Fig. 6). Fold cleaner in half (Fig. 7).

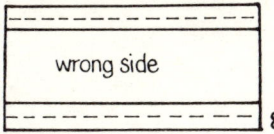

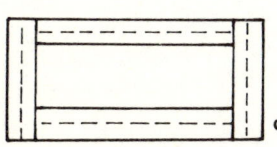

On orange cloth turn over each long side on to wrong side (Fig. 8). Tack down.

Turn over each short side (Fig. 9). Tack down.

Lay pipe-cleaner along tail (Fig. 10).

Fold tail in half, so that pipe-cleaner is inside (Fig. 11). Right side of cloth is now outside. Oversew edges together. Remove tacking threads.

Twist tail round stuffing stick or thick pencil to make it curl (Fig. 12).

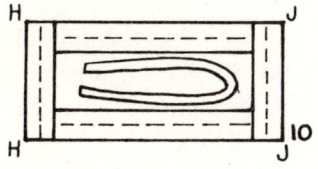

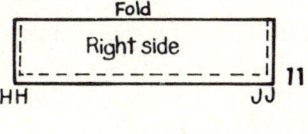

Using thread double, ladder stitch end of tail to body. See position marked on body pattern. Sew round twice.

Rory Lion

MATERIALS

Fine orange woollen cloth, 48 cm × 23 cm (19 in × 9 in); orange nylon net, for mane, four pieces each 45 cm × 5 cm (18 in × 2 in) and one piece, for tail tuft, 9 cm × 5 cm (3½ in × 2 in); *thread*, machine twist, orange, stranded cotton, black; kapok or soft cotton flock.

PATTERN

Body. Take a sheet of paper 24 cm × 12 cm. Rule lines across it and down it 2 cm apart. Copy the pattern on to these lines (see page 18). Cut out. Cut two pieces in orange cloth.
Legs and Ears. Trace patterns. Cut four forelegs, four back legs and four ears in orange cloth.

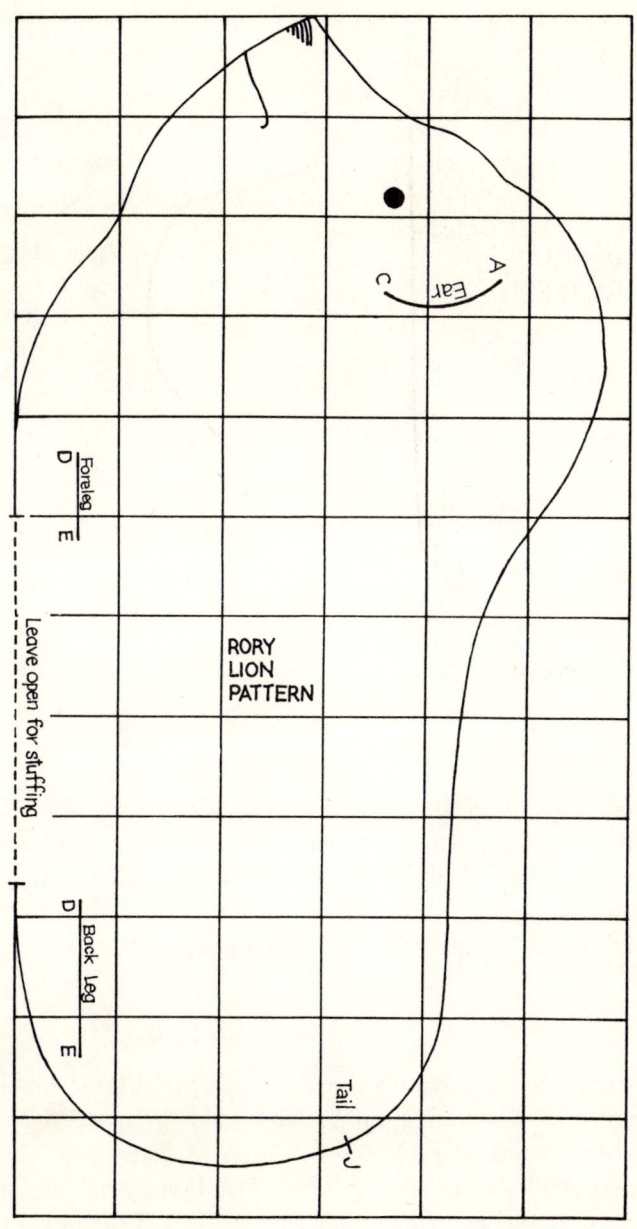

RORY
LION
PATTERN

Foreleg

D — E

Leave open for stuffing

Back Leg

D — E

Tail

Ear

A C

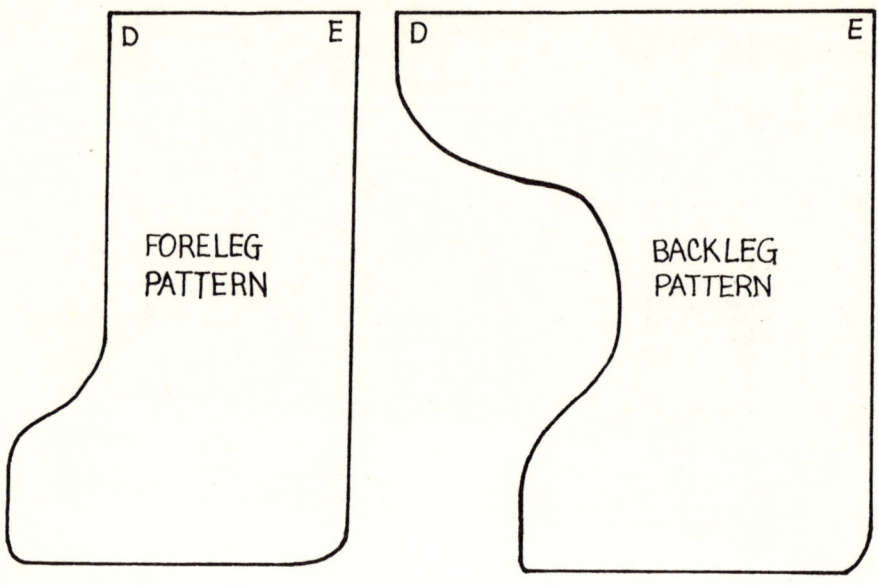

Tail. Cut one piece, 6 cm × 3 cm (2½ in × 1¼ in) in orange.

BODY

Pin the two pieces together, with wrong sides to outside. Backstitch, 6 mm (¼ in) from edge, with orange thread used double. Leave opening for stuffing, see position marked on pattern. Round the opening turn edges over to wrong side and tack down. Turn to right side. Stuff. Use thread double and ladder stitch to close opening.

EARS

For each ear pin two pieces together, with wrong sides to outside. Backstitch, 6 mm (¼ in) from edge, along AB and BC. Round AC turn edges over to wrong side and tack down. Turn to right side. Take a few stitches along AC to close the opening. Use thread double and gather along AC. Draw gathers up slightly and fasten off thread. Pin one ear

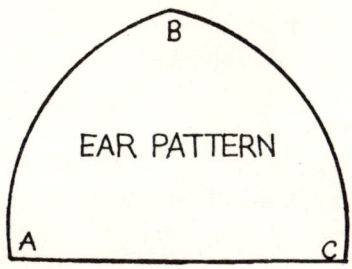

EAR PATTERN

on each side of head, see position on body pattern. Using thread double, ladder stitch twice round AC.

FEATURES

All done in black stranded cotton, 3 strands. See position on body pattern.

Eyes. Satin stitch.

Nose. Triangle in satin stitch. Figure shows front view. One straight stitch to mouth.

Mouth. Stem stitch.

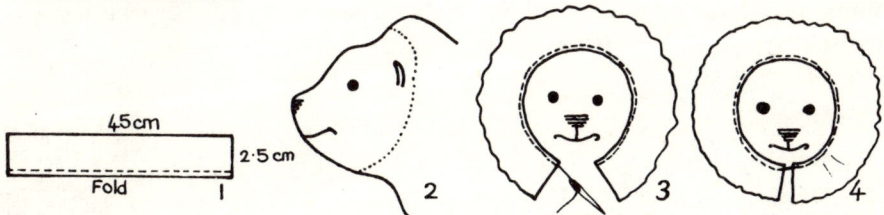

MANE

Fold one strip of net in half lengthways (Fig. 1). Using orange thread double gather along the edge as close to the fold as possible. See dotted line on Figure 1. Do not finish off thread. Put mane round head, immediately behind ears, with ends under chin. See dotted line on Figure 2. Take thread that is hanging and put it through start of gathers to pull ends of mane together (Figures 3 and 4). Pull thread tight. This pulls mane to exact size needed to fit firmly. Take a few stitches through ends of mane to finish off thread. Arrange gathers evenly all round head. Using thread double, ladder stitch right round mane to attach it to body.

Repeat with remaining three strips of net, placing each one close behind the previous one. As each strip of mane is double net, gently separate each layer to get the frilliest effect.

LEGS

For each foreleg and each back leg pin two pieces together, with wrong sides to outside. Backstitch, 6 mm ($\frac{1}{4}$ in) from edge, with thread used double. Leave DE open for stuffing. Round DE, turn edges over to wrong side and tack down. Turn to right side. A stuffing stick helps to turn out the foreleg. Stuff. Leave open.

Sew two legs to each side of body. See position marked on body pattern. Easiest way is to hold lion upside down while sewing legs. Use thread double and ladder stitch twice round DE.

Bracing Legs. To make toy stand steadily brace each leg. With toy still upside down hold leg in a straight upright position. With thread used single do an extra row of ladder stitch between inside of leg and body to keep leg in this position.

TAIL

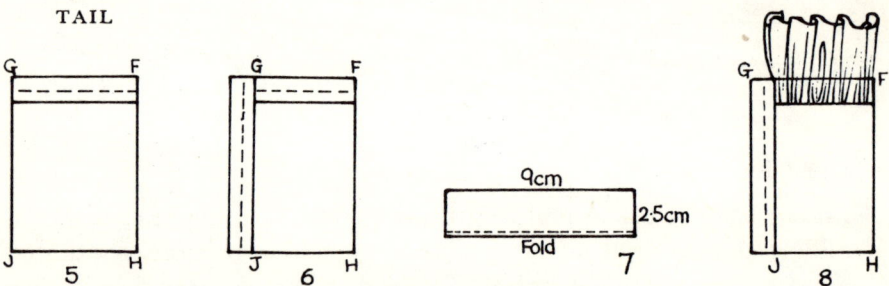

On orange cloth turn over one short side on to wrong side (Fig. 5). Tack down. Turn over one long side (Fig. 6). Tack down.

Fold orange net for tuft in half. Use thread double and gather along folded edge. See dotted line on Figure 7. Pin start of gathers to F, on

84

wrong side. Pull up gathers to make net finish at G (Fig. 8). Finish off thread to fix gathers and stitch net firmly along FG. If net is sewn through turned over bit of cloth, no stitches will show on right side.

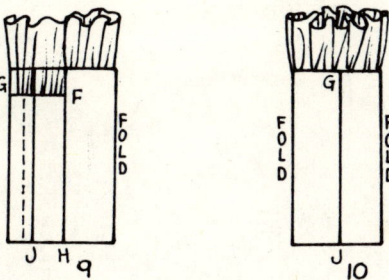

Fold FH over to middle of tail (Fig. 9). Fold GJ over on top of it (Fig. 10). Right side is now to outside. Using thread double, ladder stitch or oversew along GJ.

Using thread double, ladder stitch end of tail, J, to body. See position on body pattern. Raw edges will be tucked inside as sewing proceeds. Sew round twice. Do an extra row of stitches under the tail to make tail slope downwards.

Rattles

Two pieces of material sewn together, with a rattle tin and stuffing in them, make a rattle. Instructions are given for circular rattles, bell-shaped rattles and ideas for variations.

BASIC INSTRUCTIONS

MATERIALS

Circular Rattle. Felt or cotton, 2 circles each 15 cm (6 in) in diameter, or draw round a saucer.

Bell Rattle. Felt, two pieces each 19 cm × 16 cm (7½ in × 6¼ in).

Both, Thread. Machine twist to match cotton; to match or contrast with felt as desired; kapok or soft cotton flock.

Rattle Tin. Small tin with lid; a few small stones; odd piece of material, any colour or thickness, and thread.

PATTERNS

Circular Rattle. Already cut.

Bell Rattle. Take a piece of paper 20 cm × 16 cm and fold it in half. It now measures 20 cm × 8 cm. Rule lines across it and down it 2 cm apart. Copy the pattern on to these lines (see page 18). Cut out to make shape as figure 1. Cut two pieces in felt.

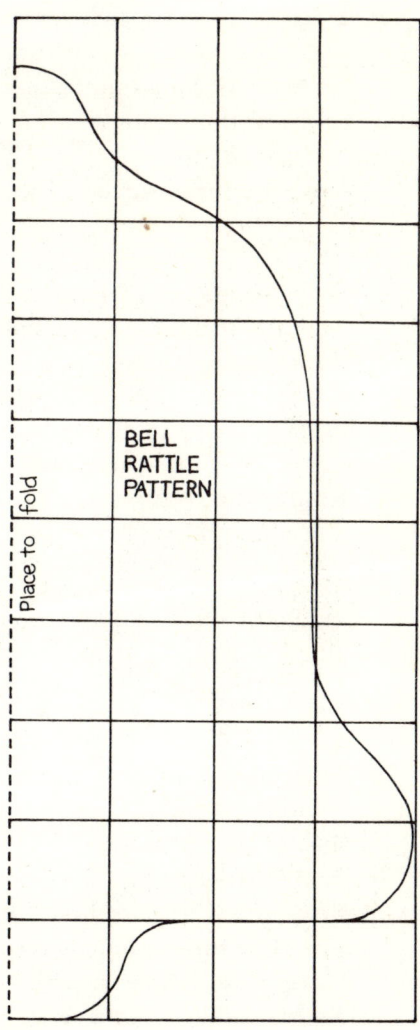

BELL
RATTLE
PATTERN

Place to fold

This may be an empty ointment, Vaseline, or similar small-sized tin. Do not go bigger than a typewriter ribbon tin. A strong plastic box such as is used for face cleansing pads makes a satisfactory rattle, though tin makes a louder noise.

Put three or four small stones in the tin, shut the lid and rattle. If it sounds dull the stones may be too big to move freely or you may have put in too many.

Wrap the tin in the odd piece of material and stitch it down.

ASSEMBLY

1. Sew two pieces of material together, using machine twist double. Sew about three-quarters of the way round to leave an opening for stuffing (Figs. 2 and 3).
   Felt. Sew on right side with stab-stitch, 3 mm ($\frac{1}{8}$ in) from edge, oversewing or blanket stitch.
   Cotton. Sew on wrong side with backstitch, 6 mm ($\frac{1}{4}$ in). from edge. Round the opening, turn edges over to wrong side and tack down. Turn to right side.

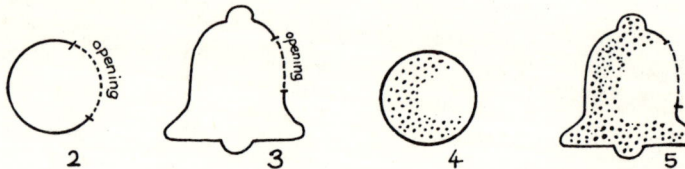

2. Put a little stuffing inside round the edge. See dotted parts on Figures 4 and 5.
3. Slip in the rattle tin.
4. Add a little stuffing over top and bottom of tin to make it feel soft.
5. Sew up half the stuffing hole.
   Felt. Use same stitch as rest of rattle.
   Cotton. Use ladder stitch.
6. Finish stuffing and sew to close opening.

Warning. Be careful with the stuffing. Keep the rattle feeling soft and do not force in so much stuffing that the result is a hard ball.

VARIATIONS ON RATTLES

1. Circular Rattle. Patterned cotton

Make the circular rattle in gaily patterned cotton. No extra adornment is required. If circles are cut from dressmaking cuttings and home-made stuffing is used, rattles will only cost a few needlefuls of thread.

2. Circular rattle. Embroidery

Choose any embroidery transfer that has child appeal. Iron transfer on to one circle of felt or plain cotton. Embroider it. Then make up rattle, following Basic Instructions, page 87.

3. Circular rattle. Felt animal

Make circular rattle in felt or plain cotton following Basic Instructions, page 87. Trace animal pattern, or draw any pattern yourself. Cut out in black felt. Use Copydex adhesive to stick it to centre of rattle.

Dog. Embroider yellow stitches for eye before sticking dog to rattle.

Cat. Embroider black whiskers after sticking cat to rattle.

Rabbit. Embroider white tail before sticking rabbit to rattle and black whiskers after sticking.

4. Circular rattle. Funny face

Cut features in scraps of felt and sew to one circle of felt before making up rattle. As features can be quaint and amusing even people who feel they cannot draw can design their own. Patterns and details are given for those who wish them.

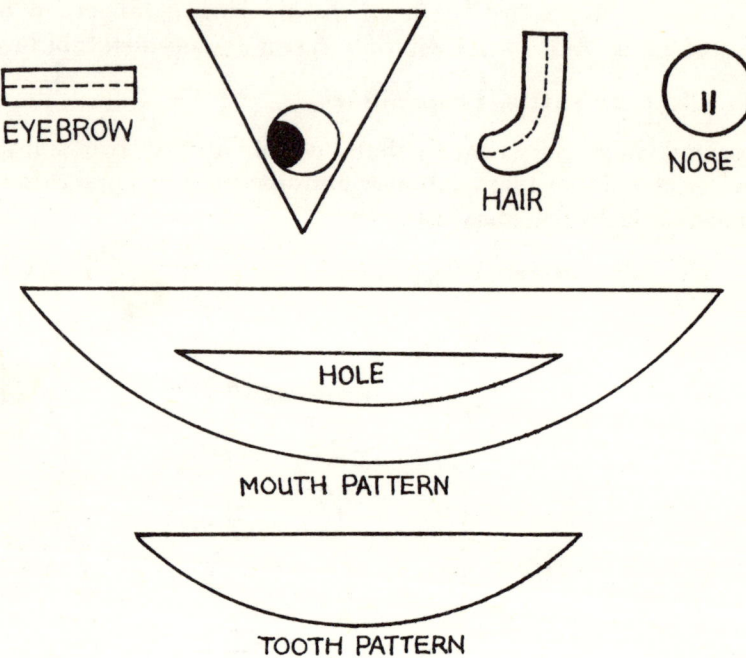

EYEBROW

HAIR

NOSE

HOLE

MOUTH PATTERN

TOOTH PATTERN

PATTERNS

Trace patterns. *White felt:* Cut two triangles for eyes and one tooth piece. *Black felt:* Cut two small circles for eyes, two eyebrows, five hair pieces and one nose. *Grass green felt:* Cut two larger circles for eyes and one mouth. Note hole in middle of mouth.

FEATURES

Eyes. Arrange pieces as shown on pattern. Use orange thread double and stitch together through centre of black circle. Sew eyes to face with white thread, running stitch, 3 mm ($\frac{1}{8}$ in) from edge (Fig. 6).

Eyebrows and *Hair*. Sew to face with black thread, backstitch. See pattern. Arrange hair to form fringe.

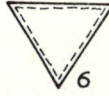 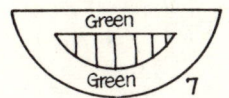

Nose. Black thread, straight stitches in centre. See pattern.

Mouth. Lay white piece on face then green on top. White shows through hole. Mark teeth on white with ballpen (Fig. 7). One line must come in centre. Cover lines with straight stitches in black. Grass-green thread, slipstitch round inside and outside of mouth.

ASSEMBLY

Make up rattle, following Basic Instructions, page 87. Opening is neatest if made beside hair.

5. Do-it-yourself shape

Design the shape of your rattles yourself. No drawing skill is needed.

PATTERN

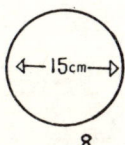  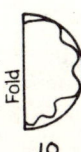 

Take a circle of paper, 15 cm (6 in) in diameter (Fig. 8). Fold it in half (Fig. 9). Draw a wavy line (Fig. 10). Just scribble an irregular line and do not indent the waves too much or there will not be room for the rattle tin in the centre. Cut out and open out to make shape (Fig. 11). Cut out two pieces in felt.

91

Anything you like. Or try a Do-it-Yourself embroidery design as illustrated.

Front of Rattle   Back of Rattle

Front of Rattle. Centre, star shape made by four straight lines crossing each other. Two lines of stem stitch surround the star. Easy way to keep lines even, is to cut smaller paper patterns than for the rattle, trace round them in pencil, then embroider on the pencil line.
Back of Rattle. One line of stem stitch embroidered near the edge.

ASSEMBLY

Make up rattle, following Basic Instructions, page 87.

6. Bell rattle. Felt strips

Three strips of felt decorate each side of the bell, which is made in felt. A Christmas bell is effective made in red felt with green and yellow strips.

Cut strips of felt, each approx. 11 cm to 12 cm ($4\frac{1}{4}$ in to $4\frac{3}{4}$ in) long and 6 mm ($\frac{1}{4}$ in) wide. Four green strips and two yellow strips make the Christmas bell. Lay three strips on each bell piece, leaving a narrow gap between each colour. Slipstitch along each side of each strip. If time is short, only top of each strip need be sewn.

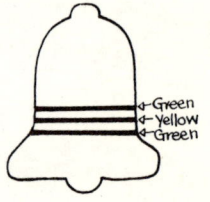

Make up rattle, following Basic Instructions, page 87, using oversewing in red.

7. Bell rattle. Ric-rac

Two pieces of ric-rac braid decorate each side of the bell, which is made in felt.

Cut 64 cm (25 in) of ric-rac in four pieces each 16 cm (6¼ in) long. Lay two pieces on each bell piece, leaving about 1 cm (½ in) between them (Fig. 12). Turn surplus at each edge over to wrong side. Tack down.

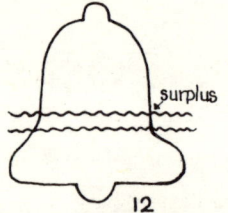

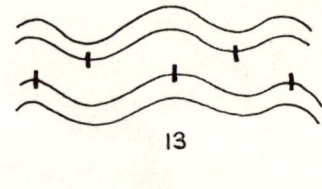

Sew down ric-rac with matching thread. Take a small straight stitch on each inner curve (Fig. 13), carrying the thread along on the wrong side.

Make up rattle, following Basic Instructions, page 87, oversewing in colour to match bell.

8. Bell rattle. Embroidery

Rows of embroidery in chain stitch decorate each side of the bell, which is made in felt. Green and gold embroidery on a mauve bell is unusual and effective.

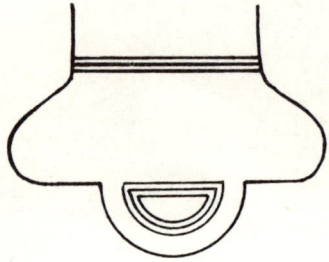

Use stranded cotton, 2 strands. Chain stitch. Embroider three lines across each bell piece and round clapper. Lines in green, gold, green, all just touching each other. To keep lines straight draw first line across bell in ball pen. Sew over it, then add the other two lines. On clapper sew outer line first, about 3 mm ($\frac{1}{8}$ in) from edge, then the other two lines just inside it.

Make up rattle, following Basic Instructions, page 87, oversewing in colour to match bell.

9. Bluebell rattle

This dainty bluebell flower is a variation on the bell-shaped rattle.

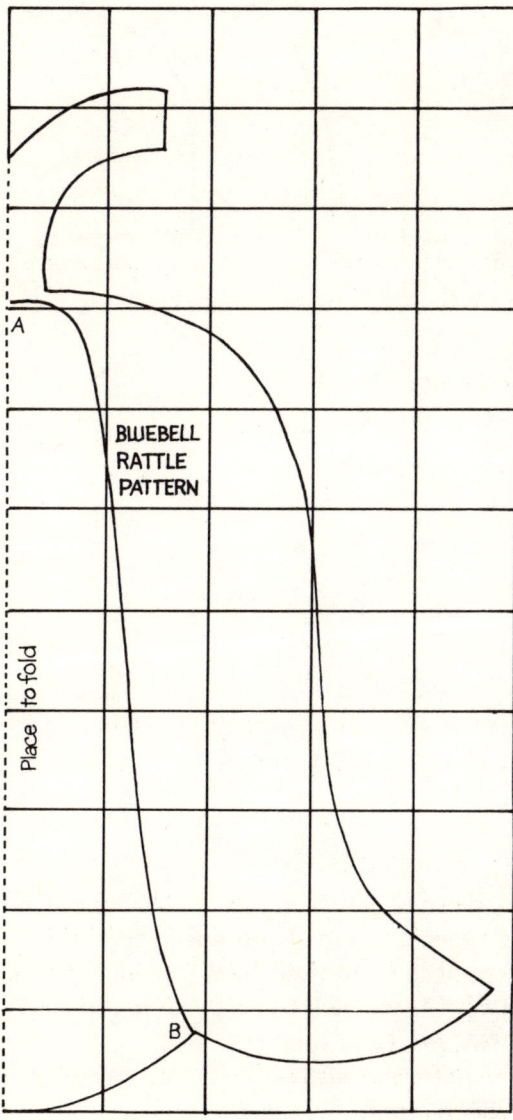

A

BLUEBELL
RATTLE
PATTERN

Place to fold

B

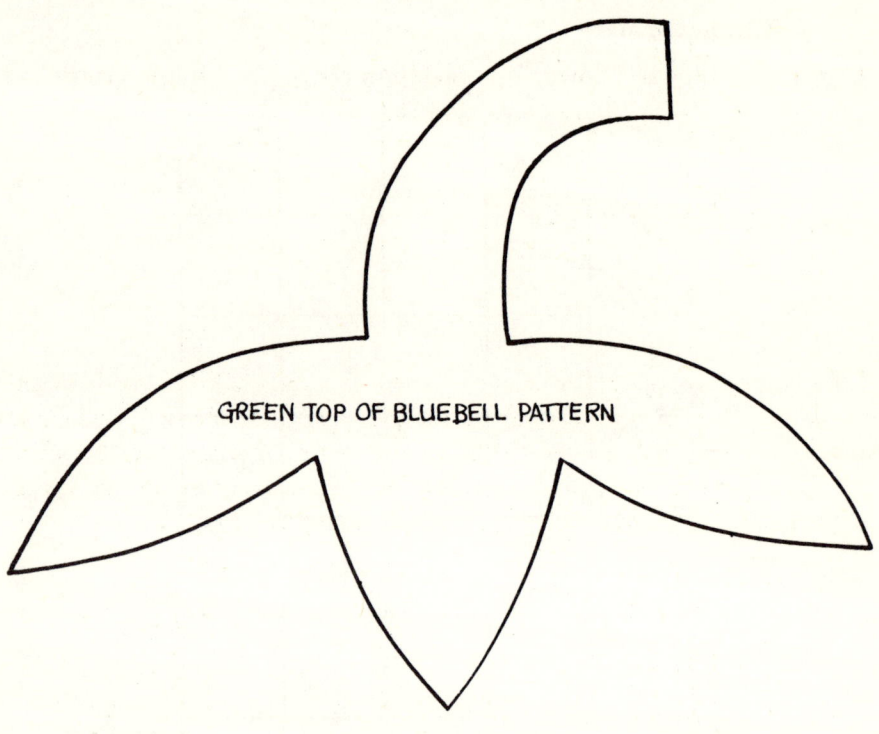

GREEN TOP OF BLUEBELL PATTERN

Pale blue felt, two pieces each 22 cm (9 in) square; green felt, two pieces each 12 cm × 10 cm (4¾ in × 4 in); *thread*, machine twist, pale blue and green; kapok or soft cotton flock; rattle tin (see page 88).

PATTERNS

Bluebell. Take a piece of paper 22 cm × 20 cm and fold it in half. It now measures 22 cm × 10 cm. Rule lines across it and down it 2 cm apart. Copy the pattern on to these lines (see page 18). Cut out to make shape as Figure 14. Cut away shaded portion of stalk to leave shape as Figure 15. Cut two pieces in blue felt.

Green Top. Trace pattern. Cut two pieces in green felt. Stalk is thicker than blue stalk as it has to fit over it.

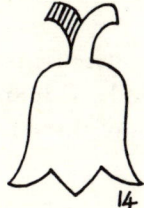  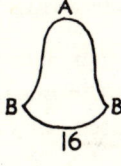

PETALS

Fold bluebell paper pattern again and draw line AB. Cut pattern and open out to make shape as Figure 16. Lay on one bluebell and *lightly* trace sides with ballpen. Stem stitch, with blue thread, along these lines to mark petals. Repeat on second bluebell but working with stalk pointing in opposite direction to make pair (Fig. 17).

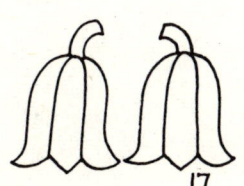  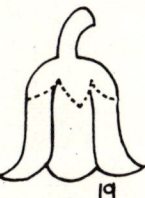

ASSEMBLY

Pin one green part on top of each bluebell on the right side (Fig. 18). Tack down. Pin the two bluebells together, with right sides to outside. Make up rattle, following Basic Instructions for Bell Rattle, page 87, using oversewing in blue, round flower, and green round top. When sewing green, try to take needle through all four thicknesses. Pointed edge of green, dotted in Figure 19, is left unsewn. No stuffing is needed in stalk.

10. Harlequin rattle

This rattle can use up small pieces of felt left over when cutting out felt toys, as there are four different colours on each side. If home-made stuffing is used, rattles will only cost a few needlefuls of thread.

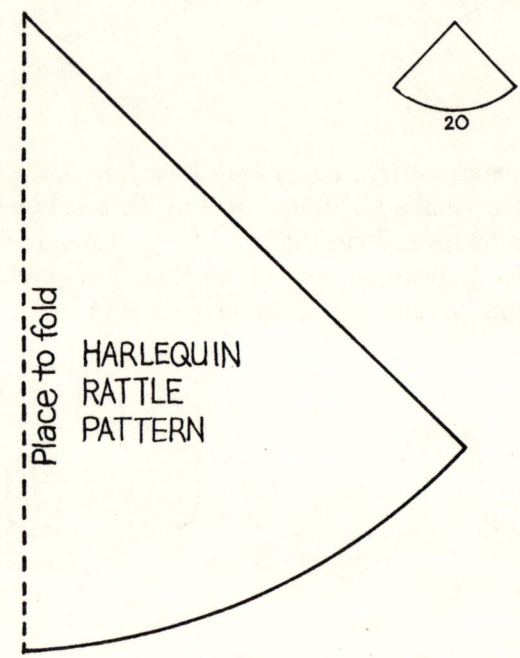

20

Place to fold

HARLEQUIN
RATTLE
PATTERN

PATTERN

Trace pattern on to folded paper. Cut out to make shape as Figure 20. Cut eight pieces in brightly coloured felts.

ASSEMBLY

Machine twist, used double. Oversewing.

Sew two pieces together, dotted line on Figure 21. Open out to make half a side (Fig. 22). Repeat with other six pieces. Pin two half-

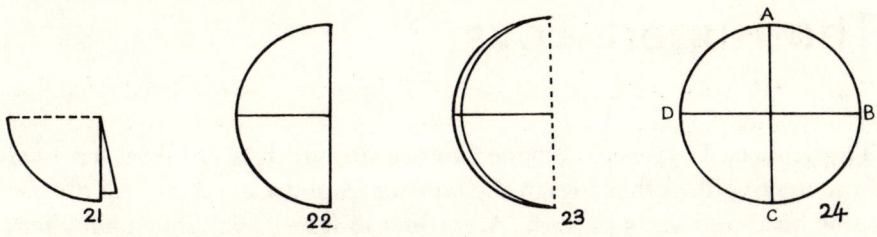

sides together, with wrong sides (that is, side showing stitching) to outside. Sew together, dotted line on Figure 23. Open out to make one side (Fig. 24). Repeat with other two half-sides.

Pin the two sides together, right sides to outside. Most professional effect is gained by matching points ABCD on front and back.

Make toy following Basic Instructions, page 87, using oversewing in black thread, to give a decorative finish on the outside.

The Rupert Toys

The Rupert Toys were designed to use up odd bits of fabric left over from making the other toys in the book or from dressmaking. All use the same head and body pattern. According to fabric available make them into different characters by changing colours and fabrics and adding different ears and features.

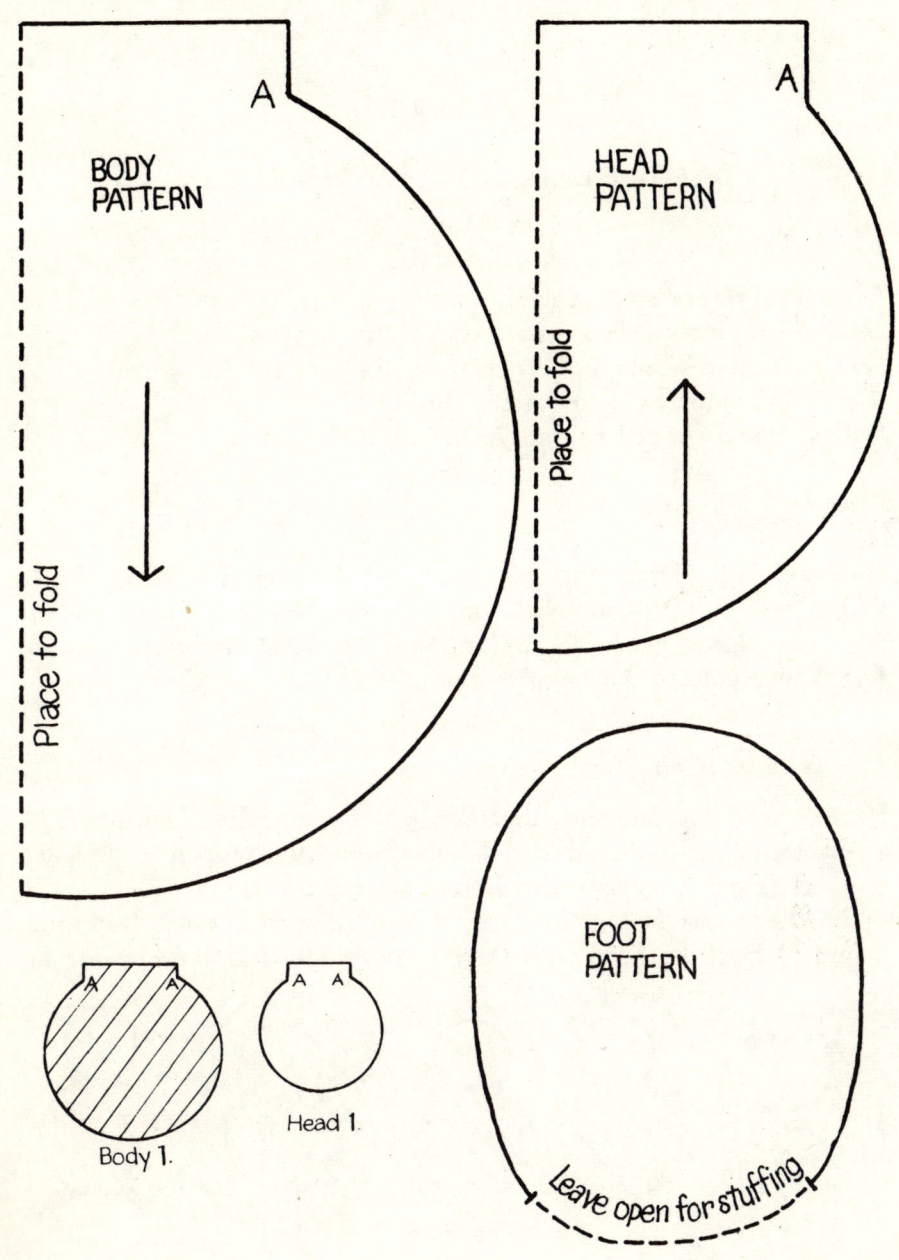

BODY PATTERN

A

Place to fold

HEAD PATTERN

A

Place to fold

A A

A A

Body 1.

Head 1.

FOOT PATTERN

Leave open for stuffing

RUPERT

BASIC HEAD, BODY AND FEET

MATERIALS

Body. Two pieces each 14 cm × 12 cm (5½ in × 4¾ in).
Head. Two pieces each 10 cm × 9 cm (4 in × 3½ in).
Feet. Four pieces each 7 cm × 6 cm (2¾ in × 2¼ in).
Thread. Machine twist to match fabrics.
Stuffing. Kapok or soft cotton, flock.

PATTERN

Head and *Body*. Trace patterns on to folded paper. Cut out to make shapes as Figure 1. Cut two bodies and two heads in fabric. For fur fabric lay pattern with pile stroking in direction of arrows on pattern.
Feet. Trace pattern. Cut four feet in fabric.

HEAD AND BODY

Pin one head and one body together, with wrong sides to outside (Fig. 2). Backstitch, with thread used double, from A to A. Open out to make one side (Fig. 3). Repeat with second head and body pieces.

Pin the two sides together, with wrong sides to outside. Backstitch 6 mm (¼ in) from edge with thread used double. Leave opening for

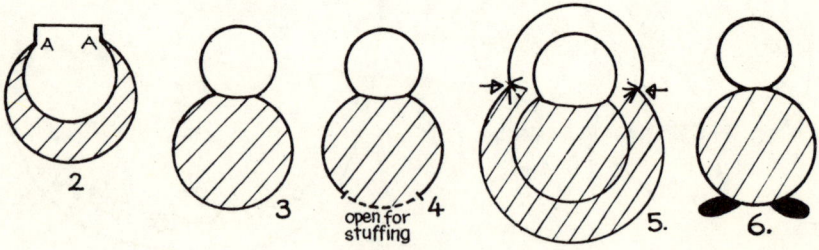

stuffing at foot (Fig. 4). Round the opening, turn edges over to wrong side and tack down. Make small cuts between sewing and edge of material at neck (Fig. 5), to let fabric turn out smoothly. Turn to right side. Stuff, making sure that neck is stuffed firmly. Use thread double and ladder stitch to close opening.

FEET

Pin two feet together, with wrong sides to outside. Backstitch, 6 mm ($\frac{1}{4}$ in) from edge with thread used double. Leave opening for stuffing at one end, see position marked on pattern. Round the opening, turn edges over to wrong side and tack down. Turn to right side. Stuff, keeping foot fairly flat and not putting in sufficient stuffing to make a balloon shape! Use thread double and ladder stitch to close opening. Repeat with remaining two feet.

Sew feet to base of body. Using thread double, ladder stitch twice along back of heel and across front of foot (Fig. 6).

RUPERT DUCK

Make Body and Head, following Rupert, Basic Instructions, page 102. Body is in patterned cotton and head in yellow fur fabric.

ADDITIONAL MATERIALS

Feet and *Bill*. Six small pieces of orange woollen cloth; *thread*, machine twist, yellow, orange, and to match body, stranded cotton, black.

PATTERN

Feet and *Bill*. Trace patterns. Cut four feet and two bills in orange.

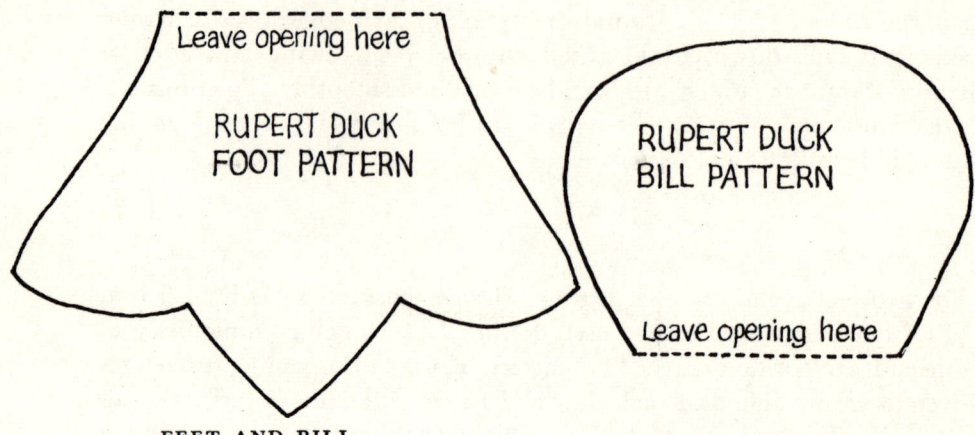

FEET AND BILL

Pin two pieces together with wrong sides to outside. Backstitch, 6 mm ($\frac{1}{4}$ in) from edge. Leave opening for stuffing on straight edge, see position marked on pattern. Round the opening turn edges over to wrong side and tack down. Turn to right side. Stuff feet lightly, stuff bill just enough to give firmness. Ladder stitch to close opening.

Feet. Sew to base of body. Using thread double, ladder stitch twice round straight edge. First time round, foot will hang down a little. Second time round, hold foot at right angles to body and the stitching across the front will hold it in that position.

Bill. Sew to front of face. Using thread double, ladder stitch twice round straight edge.

EYES

Black stranded cotton, 4 strands.

Three or four straight stitches to raise eye above fur.	Satin stitch across them for three or four layers or until eye is prominent.	Orange thread used double. Three small stitches in centre of eye.

RUPERT CAT

Make Body, Head and Feet, following Rupert, Basic Instructions, page 102. Body is in royal blue cotton, head and feet in orange woollen cloth.

ADDITIONAL MATERIALS

Orange woollen cloth, four small pieces for ear, one piece 14 cm × 2 cm (5½ in × ¾ in) for tail; scraps of felt in white and grass green; *thread*, machine twist, royal blue, orange and black; Copydex adhesive; ribbon 36 cm (15 in) long.

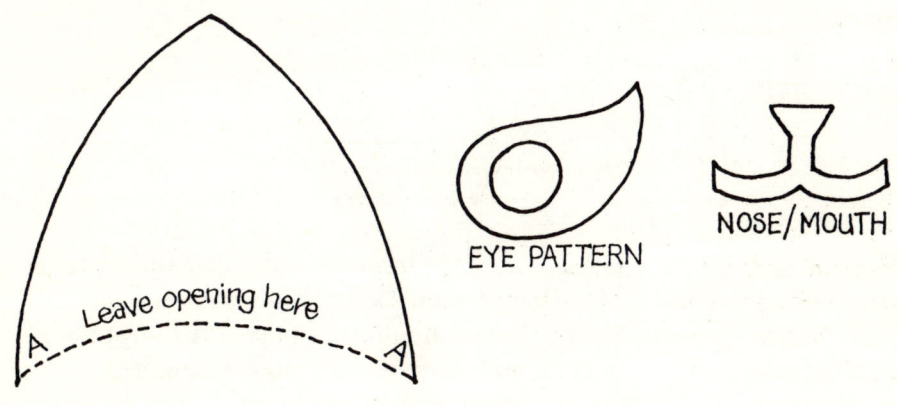

EYE PATTERN

NOSE/MOUTH

Leave opening here

PATTERN

Ears. Trace pattern. Cut four in orange.
Eyes and *Nose/Mouth*. Trace patterns. Cut two large eyes in white felt, two small circles for eyes and one nose/mouth piece in grass green felt.

EARS

For each ear pin two pieces together, with wrong sides to outside. Back-stitch, 6 mm (¼ in) from edge, leaving opening at foot, see position marked on pattern. Round the opening turn edges over to wrong side and tack down. Turn to right side. Take a few stitches to close the opening.

Bring the two points, A, to meet and take a stitch to join them (Fig. 7). Place an ear on each side of head, along top seam (Fig. 8). Using thread double, ladder stitch twice round foot of ear.

TAIL

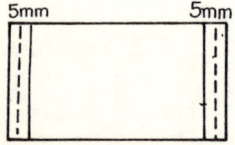

Turn over short edges about 5 mm. Tack down.

Turn over each long side about 5 mm. Tack down. Edges should meet along centre.

Fold in half, bringing points AB to meet. All tacked turnings are now on inside.

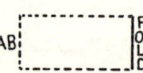

Oversew or ladder stitch the three edges, shown dotted.

Place on back of cat. Using thread double, ladder stitch twice round short end AB.

106

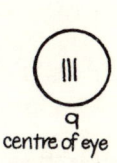

centre of eye

FEATURES

Eyes. Place green circle on white eye. Use black thread double and stitch together through centre of green circle, with straight upright stitches (Fig. 9). Make second eye in reverse direction to form a pair (Fig. 10). Use Copydex to stick to face.
Nose/Mouth. Use Copydex to stick to face (Fig. 10).
Whiskers. Black thread. Use stem stitch to mark three whiskers each side of nose.

RIBBON

Tie ribbon round neck and make bow at front.

RUPERT RABBIT

Make Body, Head and Feet, following Rupert, Basic Instructions, page 102. Body in patterned cotton, head in white cotton and feet in black cotton.

ADDITIONAL MATERIALS

Ears. Two pieces white cotton, two pieces blue cotton and two pieces Vilene interlining, each 13 cm × 5 cm (5 in × 2 in); yellow nylon net, three strips each 40 cm × 5 cm (16 in × 2 in) for neck and two strips each 10 cm × 2 cm (4 in × ¾ in) for feet; scraps of light brown felt;

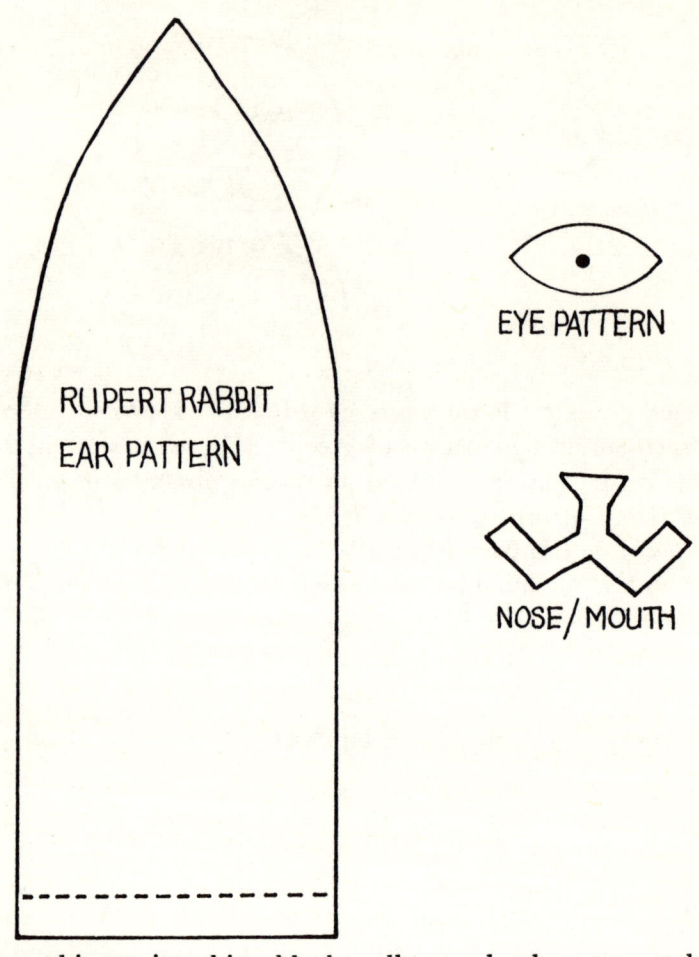

RUPERT RABBIT
EAR PATTERN

EYE PATTERN

NOSE/ MOUTH

thread, machine twist white, black, yellow and colour to match body; Copydex adhesive.

Hint. Ear linings and net look effective in colours picked out from pattern on body cotton.

PATTERN

Ears. Trace pattern. Cut two in white and two in blue. Cut two in Vilene only as far as dotted line.

Eyes and *Nose/Mouth*. Trace patterns. Cut two eyes and one nose/mouth in light brown felt.

ROSETTES ON FEET

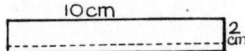 

| Gather one long side of a strip of net. Use thread double. Sew near edge. | Pull up gathers tightly. Finish off thread. Stitch end to start to form rosette. | Sew to front of foot near toe. Use thread double. Ladder stitch round twice. |

EARS

For each ear place one blue and white ear together, with wrong sides to outside. Lay Vilene ear on top of white. Pin all together. Backstitch, 6 mm ($\frac{1}{4}$ in) from edge, leaving opening across foot. Round the opening turn edges over to wrong side and tack down. Turn to right side, turning between the blue and white ears. Take a few stitches to close the opening. With blue side facing forwards bring the two points to meet at centre (Fig. 11). Use white thread double and stitch the two points together, then ladder stitch ear to top of head, sewing round twice. Blue lining faces to front.

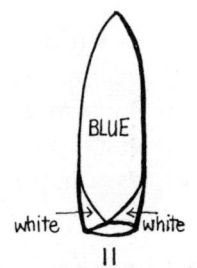

FEATURES

Eyes. Yellow thread, used double. Embroider satin stitch spot in centre of each eye.
Eyes and *Nose/Mouth*. Stick to face with Copydex.

Pin the three long strips of net on top of each other. Gather one long side, using thread double. Sew near edge. Put round neck. Take thread through starting point and pull up tightly to fit neck. Stitch to fix it and finish off thread. Join should come at back of neck. Stitching does not go through rabbit. Arrange gathers evenly round neck. Gently pull apart the three layers of net.

RUPERT FUNNIMAN

Make Body, Head and Feet, following Rupert, Basic Instructions, page 102. Body is in black and white check gingham, head in pink cotton and feet in black cotton.

ADDITIONAL MATERIALS

Scraps of felt in grass green for collar, yellow for tie, red, white, blue and black for features; *thread*, machine twist in white, pink, black, yellow and green; Copydex adhesive; rug wool in green, or any bright colour that is not a natural hair colour, twelve lengths each 15 cm (6 in) long; tissue paper, two pieces each 10 cm × 3 cm (4 in × 1¼ in).

FEATURES

EYE
2 white

EYE
2 blue

EYEBROW
4 black

NOSE
1 red

MOUTH . 1 red

12

Trace patterns. Cut in felt.

Place blue eye on white eye. Yellow thread double, stitch through centre (Fig. 12). Stick all features to face with Copydex (Fig. 12).

HAIR

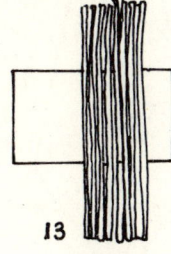

13

Lay rug wool across one piece of tissue paper, (Fig. 13). Crowd it into a 4 cm (1½ in) area putting strands double.

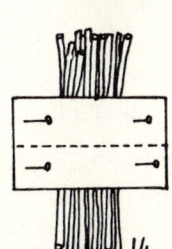

14

Pin second piece of tissue paper on top. Use green thread double. Backstitch along middle (Fig. 14). This forms the parting in the hair. Remove pins. Tear away the under layer of tissue.

15

Place wig on head, with parting in centre (Fig. 15). Use green thread double. Backstitch along parting, taking stitches through head. Tear away the top layer of tissue.

16   17

At centre back of head there will be a gap (Fig. 16). Use green thread to stitch strands of hair together to close gap (Fig. 17). Hair at centre back will now be too long. Trim as necessary.

COLLAR AND TIE

Trace patterns. Collar is traced on to folded paper, then opened out. Cut one collar in green felt and one tie in yellow felt.

Put Copydex on back of 'knot' of tie. Stick to body under chin. Rest

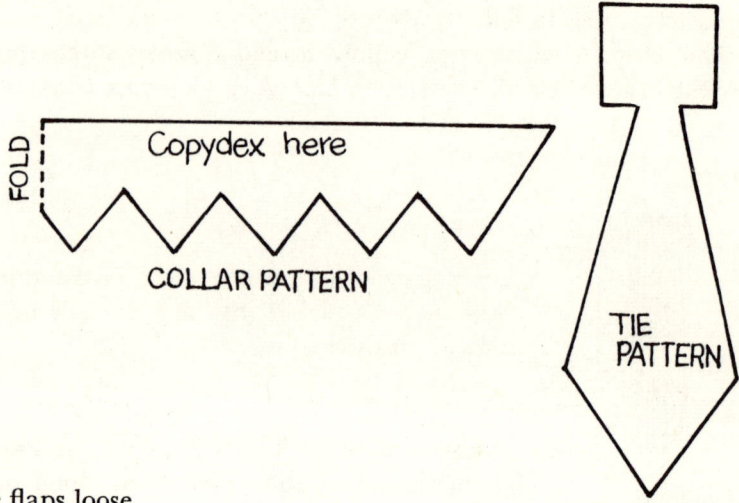

COLLAR PATTERN

TIE PATTERN

of tie flaps loose.

Try collar round neck to see where it lies neatly. Put Copydex along straight edge of collar, see pattern and stick round neck. Easiest way is to position one corner on the tie, wind collar round neck and finish with last corner on top of tie. Press firmly on tie.

RUPERT MONKEY

Body and Head are cut as Rupert, Basic Instructions, page 102, with body in turquoise cotton and head in brown fur fabric. Join body and head at neck as far as Figure 3, page 102. Leave at this stage as features and buttons are added before main sewing and stuffing are done.

ADDITIONAL MATERIALS

Tail. Brown fur fabric, 20 cm × 3 cm (8 in × 1¼ in), with pile stroking along the length.

Face. 5 cm (2 in) square yellow felt.

Ears. Two pieces each 5 cm × 4 cm (2 in × 1½ in) yellow felt.

Feet. Four pieces yellow felt and two pieces Vilene interlining each

6 cm × 4 cm (2½ in × 1½ in); scraps of light brown felt; *thread*, machine twist, turquoise, brown, yellow and red; stranded cotton, black; 3 small red buttons.

FACE

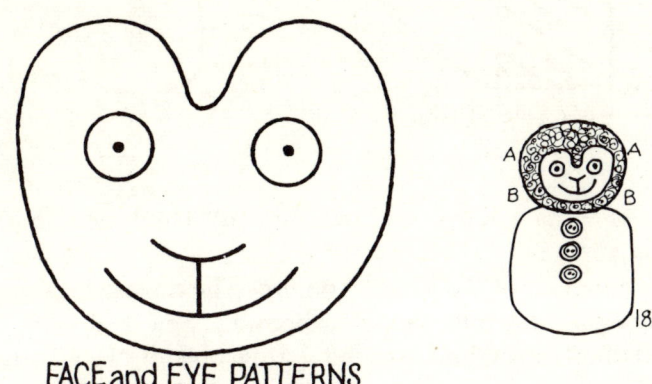

FACE and EYE PATTERNS

Trace pattern. Cut in yellow felt. Cut two circles in light brown felt for eyes. Stitch eyes to face using yellow thread double and sewing through centre of circle to form dot in middle of eye. Pencil nose and mouth. Embroider in stem stitch with black stranded cotton. Pin face to centre of head, on right side of fur fabric (Fig. 18). Use yellow thread. Slipstitch edge of face to head, making stitches as small as possible.

BUTTONS

Use red thread double. Sew the buttons to the front of the body (Fig. 18).

EARS

Trace pattern. Cut two in yellow felt.
   Lay one side of the monkey on a table, face facing upwards, as Figure 18. Lay one ear on each side of head, matching points AB on

113

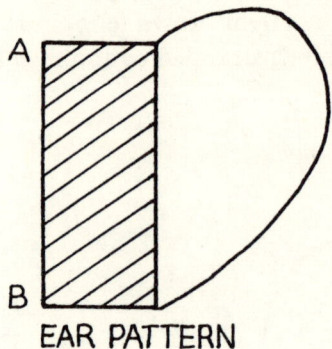

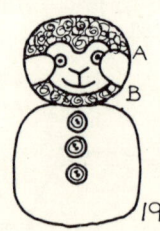

EAR PATTERN

head and ear. Ears will overlap face (Fig. 19). Hold them in place with big tacking stitches.

Pin the other side of the monkey on top. The right side faces down on to the ears and the wrong side is uppermost. Sew and stuff, following Rupert, Basic Instructions, second paragraph of 'Head and Body', page 102.

Alternative. If you prefer to sew on the ears afterwards, sew and stuff the toy as in Rupert, Basic Instructions, page 102. Cut the ear pattern without the shaded part. Use thread double and ladder stitch an ear to each side of head.

FEET

Trace pattern. Cut four in yellow felt and two in Vilene. Cut narrow border off Vilene all round to make it a little smaller than foot.

For each foot pin one Vilene between two felts. Mark toes with pencil, see pattern. Use yellow thread. Oversew round edge of foot. As toes are reached, sew them with straight stitches, going through to back of foot. Two stitches form each toe, see pattern, and sew over them two or three times.

Sew feet to base of body. Using thread double, ladder stitch twice along back of heel and across front of foot. Big toes are at inner side of feet (Fig. 20).

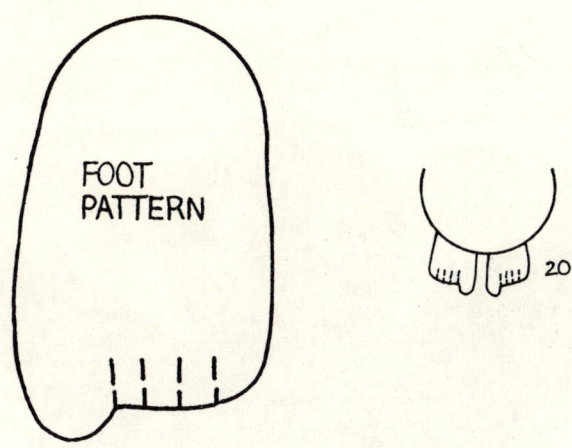

FOOT
PATTERN

20

TAIL

Make as Rupert Cat's tail. When sewing to body make fur fabric stroke from body to tip of tail. Attach tail *very firmly* to body as owner may swing monkey by its tail!

JUNGLE MONKEY

If there is sufficient brown fur fabric make the body in fur fabric and omit the buttons.

Jock McThistle

This glove puppet is simple to operate. Put thumb in one arm of the puppet, two fingers in the head and the last two fingers in the other arm.

MATERIALS

Green felt, two pieces each 30 cm × 26 cm (12 in × 10 in) *or* one piece 46 cm × 30 cm (18½ in × 12 in) if pattern is laid as Figure 1; scraps of white and red felt; *thread*, machine twist, green; mauve wool, which can

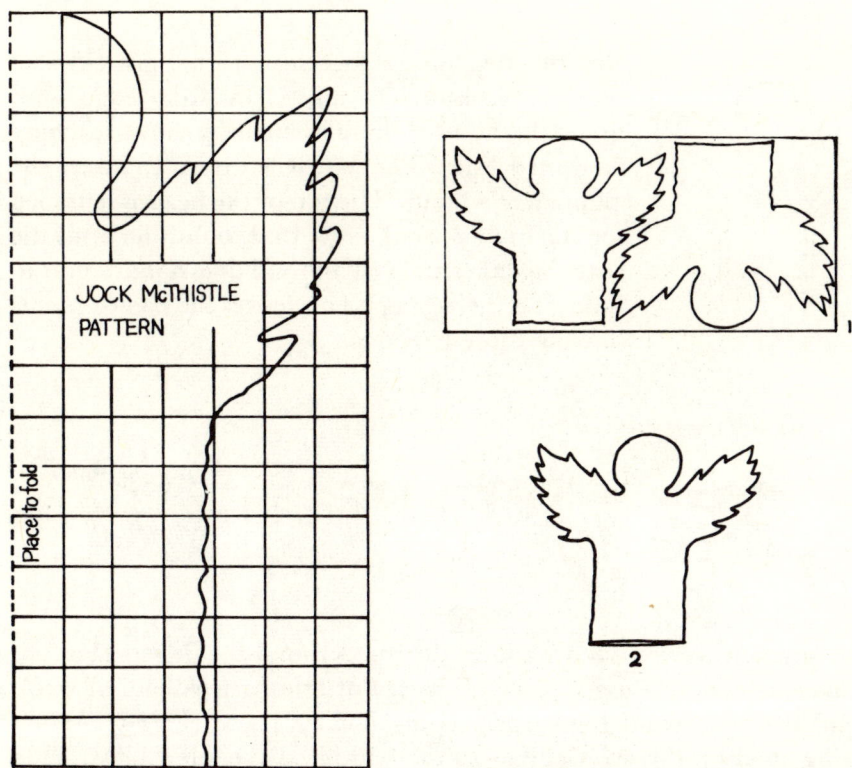

JOCK McTHISTLE
PATTERN

Place to fold

1

2

be any shade from pale mauve to reddish purple. Very thin wool looks best, but any thickness will do and any type of wool. Any quantity as mauve top of the thistle can have just a few strands or be a really thick patch; card, one piece 7 cm ($2\frac{3}{4}$ in) square; Copydex adhesive.

PATTERN

Take a sheet of paper 30 cm × 28 cm and fold it in half. It now measures 30 cm × 14 cm. Rule lines across it and down it 2 cm apart. Copy the pattern on to these lines (see page 18). Cut out to make shape as Figure 2. Cut two pieces in green felt.

Sewing Features. If you wish to sew the eyes and mouth instead of sticking them with Copydex, do it now before the sides are joined.

BODY

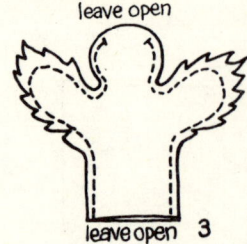

leave open

leave open 3

Pin the two pieces together, with right sides to outside. Backstitch, 6 mm ($\frac{1}{4}$ in) from edge, with green thread used double. Figure 3 shows stitching as dotted lines. The foot is left open to insert the puppeteer's hand. The top of the head is left open for the mauve wool. Note that round the arms the stitching takes an even line and does not attempt to follow all the zigzags. This leaves the jagged points looking more effective.

THE MAUVE TOP

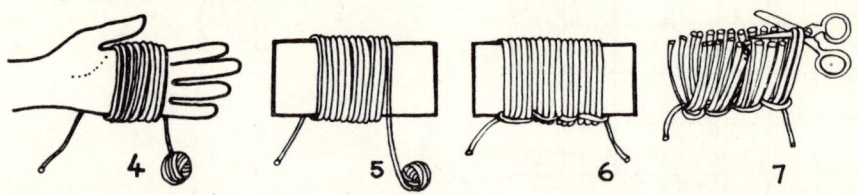

4   5   6   7

The quickest way to wind wool for the top is round the fingers (Fig. 4). It may be easier to use a piece of card. Put aside a needleful of wool. Wind the rest round the card, keeping it fairly loose (Fig. 5). When wool is used up thread needle with the odd bit. Take a few big stitches along foot of wool, just to hold it roughly together (Fig. 6). Cut along top of card to release wool (Fig. 7).

Slip the sewn end into the top of the head through the opening. Pin through both sides of felt and wool. Backstitch across the opening with green thread used double, going through all thicknesses, that is the two felts and the wool.

FEATURES

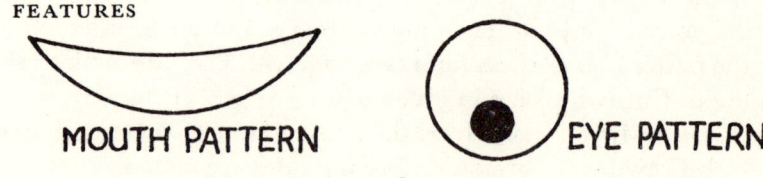

MOUTH PATTERN   EYE PATTERN

Trace patterns.

Eyes. Cut two large circles in white felt and two small circles in green felt. Use Copydex to stick the green circle to the white one, then the white one to the face.

Mouth. Cut one in red felt. Use Copydex to stick to face.